AF397967

Martin Reén

Partnering with the Love of Christ

Spiritual Disciplines & The New Covenant

© 2023 Martin Reén

Proofreading: Marie Enoksson
Publisher: Healing Streams
Print: BoD – Books on Demand, Norderstedt, Germany

ISBN: 978-91-527-3598-5

TABLE OF CONTENTS

Preface 9

Introduction 11

Part One: Developing Life in the Secret Place

Chapter 1: In the Potter's Hand 19

Chapter 2: The Power of Good Habits 29

Chapter 3: The Reward of the Secret Place 37

Chapter 4: Motivated by Love 51

Part Two: Spiritual Disciplines – Partnering with the Love of Christ

Chapter 5: Encountering Jesus through the Scriptures 61

Chapter 6: The Word of God and Our Heart 71

Chapter 7: Being a Worshipper in Spirit & Truth 83

Chapter 8: Soaking in His Presence 95

Chapter 9: Fasting to Gain Focus and Clarity 105

Chapter 10: The Blessings of Fasting in Isaiah 58 117

Chapter 11: The Joy of Intercession 125

Chapter 12: The Lifestyle & Fruit of Intercession 133

Chapter 13: Words that Impart Grace 145

Chapter 14: Dreaming with God 159

Chapter 15: Finding Mentors & Wise Guidance 171

Chapter 16: Discerning the Wisdom of Jesus 181

Chapter 17: Desire Spiritual Gifts 193

Chapter 18: A Generous Lifestyle 203

Chapter 19: Reaching the World with His Love 215

Chapter 20: Resting in Christ 229

Closing Words.. 239

Bibliography 241

About the Author... 243

PREFACE

When I wrote my previous book *Abiding in the Father's Love*, I realized that needed to cut out a lot of teaching on our life as sons and daughters, abiding in the love of the Father. Because of this, I already had in mind to write this second book, but didn't really know where to start. Around that time, I recorded an episode on my podcast on the topic of investing in our relationship with the Father.

The point I made in that episode was that if we want an intimate relationship with God, we need to invest in it. In that episode, I shared some simple thoughts and some practical advice on this topic. I received a huge amount of positive feedback from that episode. I felt how the Holy Spirit spoke to me about writing a book on this topic, which resulted in me writing this book. In my previous book, *Abiding in the Father's Love*, I laid the foundation upon which this book is built. Although not necessary, I highly recommend that you read that book first to understand more deeply the truths that this book is built upon.

Even though my focus has been - and continues to be - to preach on the love of the Father and the finished work of Christ, I love spiritual disciplines and I'm committed to build good habits to invest in my relationship with my heavenly Father. I have also seen an increasing need to address this issue, since some people who receive a revelation on the grace and love of God end up in passivity. This happens when they confuse partnering with Jesus through good habits and spiritual disciplines with legalism. This is unfortunate, because there is a big difference between being driven by guilt and a search for identity, compared to building a deeper intimacy with God by investing time and attention into our relationship with Him. The former will lead to despair and exhaustion, while the latter leads to true freedom and intimacy with Jesus Christ.

I made a commitment early in my ministry to never write or preach on topics that I do not live myself. I want to share life, not just information. Therefore, whatever topic I write on needs to be something that the Holy Spirit first has revealed to me and that has become so one with me that I live it to some degree. This is the reason why I have chosen the specific spiritual disciplines I'm writing about within the pages of this book. They have all been hugely beneficial to me and they have been a part of my journey with Jesus that I would never want to be without. My hope and prayers are that this book will be an encouragement for you as well. The Father is calling you to go deeper into His loving heart. By responding to His love, you will grow in your relationship with Christ. You'll find the true contentment and peace that only the Father can give and furthermore, a lot of people will have life transforming encounters with the love of God through you!

Your brother in Christ,
Martin Reén

INTRODUCTION

Encountering the love of God is a life changing experience and as we learn to abide in it, living loved by Him will become our life. This was the point I wanted to make in my previous book in this series, the one called *Abiding in the Father's Love*. The Father's plan for us has always been for us to learn to be good receivers of His goodness, but that does not mean that we should remain passive, however. God has placed within our hearts both a desire and an ability to respond to His love. This is because our Father desires a dynamic relationship with His children. He wants us to be both receivers and responders to the unforced rhythms of His grace. In this way, we partner with Jesus Christ, so that His life and character can be formed within us. There is such a joy and satisfaction in being able to partner with His love, which is why the title of this book is *Partnering with the Love of Christ — Spiritual Disciplines & The New Covenant*.

How Can I Build a Deep Relationship with the Father?

One common question among believers concerns how to build a deep and more intimate relationship with God. This has been my desire since the day I met Jesus, and I realize that I am not alone. I meet believers everywhere who long for a deeper relationship with the Father and I am writing this book to inspire you to grow in intimacy with Him. When writing on responding to His love, I am not, by any means, considering myself an expert on these matters. I am very much a little boy in the things of God, and I have much to learn as I continue grow in intimacy with Him. But throughout these pages, I want to share some glimpses of what I have seen so far on my journey into the depths of the Father's heart. There is no set manual on how to know God because He is a person and so are we. A rich relationship with Jesus will look very different for different people, but the Bible still has a lot to say on how we can draw near to Him. We find the true meaning of life as we make knowing Him our main purpose. This is only possible because He loved us first, and encountering His love causes us to want to respond with our whole heart (1 John. 4:19).

A Heart at Rest

"Such hope [in God's promises] never disappoints us, because God's love has been abundantly poured out within our hearts through the Holy Spirit who was given to us" (Rom. 5:5 AMP). As that love fills our hearts, we will be drawn into a deeper intimacy with Him. Jesus Christ is the deepest desire of the human heart and because we were created to love Him, our hearts will find true rest only in His presence. The heart is the core of who we are and therefore when our heart is at rest, we are at rest as well. There is no greater place to be than to live in fellowship with Jesus Christ. That is and always will be the main calling of every believer (1 Cor. 1:9).

Our Desire to Respond to His Love

The Father is always with us and His love towards us remains the same. He delights in us. He will never change, but to have an intimate relationship with God, we need quality time where we give Him our focused attention. This is the purpose of spiritual disciplines. They are pathways through which we can focus our attention on God and set our heart on Him. Spiritual disciplines have helped me to build my relationship with the Father, Jesus and the Holy Spirit in a way that helps me stay connected to the heart of God all the time. I have discovered that even though He always loves me and His presence always goes with me, I need daily reminders to be present with Him as well.

Sometimes people who have received a revelation of God's grace and the love of the Father have confused spiritual disciplines and good habits with legalistic rituals, based on doing things to earn our Father's favor. But these are totally different things. Spiritual disciplines are all about partnering with Jesus Christ, so that we can be conformed into His image. We cannot accomplish that by ourselves, but we can choose to partner with Him who can.

My Joy & Hesitation in Writing this Book

It has been such a joy for me to write this book. I can honestly say that finding ways to respond to the Father is one of the greatest pleasures of my life. This is the reason I love spiritual disciplines so much. But still, I had some hesitation when it became clear to me that this would be my next book to write. I realized that some people will almost certainly misunderstand what I am trying to communicate, thinking that building a relationship with God is about how well they perform certain disciplines. But I knew that this hesitation was based on fear, so I decided to write anyway. Abiding in the Father's love and resting in the finished work of Christ always need to be our goal as His sons and daughters.

Spiritual disciplines are biblical ways of responding to Him who loved us first, but they are never the main thing. If they become the main thing in your life, you need to lay it down and turn your focus back to living loved by the Father (1 John 4:16-19). On the other hand, we need good habits in our relationship with God to stay focused on Jesus, so that we can build a life that lasts and grows stronger together with Him.

Being Healed from the Wound of a Religious Devotional Life

A lot of people have been badly wounded in the area of spiritual disciplines because of religious teaching and legalistic advice in this area. This type of teaching and advice have been given with good intentions, but the people who were sharing them lacked revelation of the love of God. Consequently, they have done far more damage than good. Sometimes, unhealed wounds cause us to react by going to an extreme, which in this case would be to throw out spiritual disciplines altogether. Since teaching built on hurts and wounds always open the door for the root of bitterness and deception, that would be a mistake.

A far better response to being wounded is to come to the Father and get healed. If reading about spiritual disciplines causes pain to resurface in your heart, I recommend you speak to Jesus about your wounds. Jesus is our Healer and He wants to bring healing and restoration to your heart (1 Pet. 2:24-25). I know this since I needed to be healed in this area myself.

Rediscovering the Joy of Responding to His Love

Many years ago, I suffered what I would like to call a spiritual burnout. I was not burnt out in the medical sense of the word, and I still functioned well in my daily life, but I got tired in my spirit. I had been striving and struggling for so long to make my spiritual life work without success that I almost gave up. I didn't have the strength to continue anymore, but after I had hit a low point in my relationship with God, I had a deep encounter with His grace that changed my life and healed my heart. Many of the revelations I received through that encounter can be found in my book *Transformed by the Grace of God*.

For some time after going through this spiritual burnout, it was very hard for me to even pray or read the Bible, but as time went by and I was renewed in my spirit, I got a new desire to respond to His love and to invest in my relationship with the Father. I rediscovered the joy of spiritual disciplines once again. My hope is that this book could be an encouragement for you on this journey as well.

The Structure of this Book

When it comes to developing a lifestyle of partnering with His love, there are several areas that need to be addressed. Therefore, I have chosen to divide this book into two parts to make it easier for you to get an overview of how we can respond to the love of God:

a. *Part One: Developing Life in the Secret Place*
   Here we will start by looking at how the Father shapes our lives according to His purposes and we will look at the proper way for us to respond. It is obvious that many believers don't live in the will of God. We will study why some believers are able to cooperate with the will of the Father and why some are not. In this section we will also look at our motivation, the power of good habits, and the reward of the secret place.

b. *Part Two: Spiritual Disciplines: Partnering with the Love of Christ*
   In this part of the book, we are going to look at how we can build a deeper relationship with the Father through spiritual disciplines. The chapters within this part of the book are devoted to providing insight on some spiritual disciplines through a new covenant lens. We will study how to partner with Jesus Christ in releasing the love of God into this world as well. As His life is being released through us, the world around us will be transformed. At the end of almost all the chapters in this part of the book, I share some advice that have helped me to practice the spiritual discipline that the chapter is addressing.

It has been exciting and challenging for me to write this book and it has provoked me to find new creative ways to partner with His love. My hope and prayers are that by reading this book you will be challenged and encouraged in the same way. The Father loves you and He longs for you to be captivated by His heart that you respond by giving your whole heart to Him in worship and holy surrender.

Part One:

Developing Life in the Secret Place

In this part of the book, we will be looking at some of the general principles of responding to the Father's love and how we can cooperate with His purpose for us. These chapters are important because they deal with God's desire for a Christlike people, as well as our motivations for responding to His love. We will also be looking at how our Father loves to reward His children and how to build our life in the secret place with God.

CHAPTER 1: IN THE POTTER´S HAND

I want to start this book by looking at a familiar episode from the book of Jeremiah, where the prophet Jeremiah is led by God to go to the potter's house to receive a prophetic word:

So I went to the potter's house, and sure enough, the potter was there, working away at his wheel. Whenever the pot the potter was working on turned out badly, as sometimes happens when you are working with clay, the potter would simply start over and use the same clay to make another pot. Then God's Message came to me: "Can't I do just as this potter does, people of Israel?" God's Decree! "Watch this potter. In the same way that this potter works his clay, I work on you, people of Israel (Jer. 18:1-5 The Message)

I love the way in which this story reveals how our Father is working with us to transform us into the people He has called us to be. It reveals His patience and mercy with us. He refuses to give up even when our lives turn out badly. When things do not turn out well for us, it is not because God is making mistakes. The failures happening in our lives are always on our side of the equation. The good news is that when we mess up, God is not throwing us away in favor of another person. He will never give up on us. Our Father loves us too much to do that, and being a quitter is not who He is. He simply starts over, and He will keep on working with us until we are where He wants us to be. God has a very clear goal in mind and He will not stop up until He gets what He wants. This refers to the individual believer as well as with His people at large. The Father has always wanted image bearers, people who reveal Jesus Christ to the world.

We Will Look Like Jesus

Our Father knew exactly what He wanted us to look like, already before He created the world:

God knew what he was doing from the very beginning. He decided from the outset to shape the lives of those who love him along the same lines as the life of his Son. The Son stands first in the line of humanity he restored. We see the original and intended shape of our lives there in him (Rom 8:29 The Message).

The Father's plan has always been to transform us into looking like Jesus. In the book, *Abiding in the Father's Love,* I spent a lot of time writing on how Christlikeness has always been His desire. I'm not going to repeat that teaching here, but for us to cooperate with the transforming work of the Holy Spirit in our lives, it is necessary to be reminded of what we are being transformed into. Jesus is the original picture and we are created in His image. We are predestined to be transformed by the power of God, in such a radical way that Christ shines forth through every area of our lives. This is impossible for us to accomplish on our own, so it must be a work of grace. The Father is the one working on us and we are to align ourselves with His dealings. As His work within us continues to transform our hearts, we will continually reveal more of Jesus Christ.

He Make our Failure Part of His Plan

Right before Paul revealed to us that we are predestined to be conformed into the image of Jesus, he made this statement: *"And we know that all things work together for good to them that love God, to them who are the called according to his purpose"* (Rom. 8:28). All things include our failures and the brokenness of our past. God is so wise and so good at shaping us into the vessel that He want us to become, that even when our lives turn out badly, He can redeem our failures into being part of His plan for our lives.

The Father doesn't cause all things that happen in our lives. There is a lot of things that can and will happen to us that are not according to His will, but He is so powerful and wise that He can make even the activities of the devil and the consequences of sin turn out for our good, if we allow Him to do so. This includes both the sins and trespasses we have committed, as well as those committed against us. Jesus is our redeemer and as He continues His work within our hearts, the end of our story will become a testimony of His goodness and grace. Through it all, Christ will be more revealed in our lives and as a result, other people's lives will be transformed by the Father's love through us. King David, despite all his flaws, or perhaps even more so, because of them, is a very good example of a life transformed by the goodness and patience of God.

King David - a Man after God's Heart

David is probably the most famous king in the history of Israel. The Lord calls him *"a man after his own heart"*. Paul is referring to this while He is preaching in the synagogue at Antioch. As Paul is speaking, he makes the following statement about king David:

"After removing Saul, he made David their king. God testified concerning him: 'I have found David son of Jesse, a man after my own heart; he will do everything I want him to do.' "From this man's descendants God has brought to Israel the Savior Jesus, as he promised (Acts 13:22-23 NIV).

This is how David is remembered today, as a man after God's own heart. David had a lot of personal challenges and there were a couple of times when David made choices that caused things to turn out bad for him. Just look at the list of some of his failures:

- David committed adultery with Bathsheba, the wife of his loyal friend Uriah and made her pregnant (2 Sam. 11:1-5).
- He lied to cover up his sin (2 Sam. 11:6-13).
- He had his friend and follower Uriah killed, just to make sure that he would not get exposed (2 Sam. 11:14-27).

These personal failures and sins of David were all connected to his adultery with Bathsheba and how he tried to cover up for his sins. This was a real low point in king David's life, but because God is good and merciful, that was not the end of the story. God sent the prophet Nathan to confront him and when he did, king David repented and God forgave him.

King David later married Bathsheba. Even though the baby from their adulterous affair died, Bathsheba became pregnant again. Through their marriage the next king was born and his name was Solomon (see 2 Sam. 11-12). Solomon became the wisest king in the history of Israel and he wrote some of the books included in the Old Testament. This is a powerful example of how the Father works like a potter on our lives. He continues His dealings with us, until our lives have been redeemed in a way that testifies of His redeeming love. God continued to favor David, making Him an example of spiritual leadership and authority, so much that Jesus Himself is sitting upon the throne of David (Luke 1:32).

The Faithfulness & Patience of God with David

God never gave up on David. The favor and honor that the Lord bestowed upon his family line is astonishing, even to the point of Jesus Himself being made a descendant of David (Matt. 1:5-6). When David sinned, he had to live with the consequences of his poor choices, but God started over again. He kept working with David until he became the man God had always wanted Him to be. Today, we remember David as a man after God's own heart. What a powerful testimony to the mercy and goodness of God!

When I have been struggling in my walk with God, the testimony of king David has been a huge comfort and encouragement. Even though things have turned out bad for me at times, I knew that the Father was not done with me yet. He is the best at restoring broken by giving second chances – even when that brokenness is the result of our own foolishness and mistakes. Our Father loves to take ordinary people like you and me and make our lives into a testimony of His redemptive power.

The Treasure within the Earthen Vessel

Failures and brokenness are part of our lives as human beings, but it reveals a lot of the humility of our Father that He is willing to work with ordinary people to accomplish His purposes. Paul addresses this when he writes: *"We are like common clay jars that carry this glorious treasure within, so that this immeasurable power will be seen as God's, not ours"* (2 Cor. 4:7 TPT). This scripture has always been a source of hope for me. Even when God is working on us and we are walking in His will, life often appear normal and unspectacular. Sometimes it will even be a bit challenging, but that doesn't mean that God is not working on us. The vessel Paul is describing here, as a picture of us, is an ordinary jar of clay, which we could compare to plastic box where we put our cookies or candy. God hides the treasure of the Kingdom within our hearts, and we live a supernatural life, because Jesus Christ now indwells us. The Father shapes our lives so that the treasure hidden within us can manifest, resulting in the Kingdom of God being revealed through our lives. This will happen in the midst of our everyday life, through our struggles and challenges.

"Though we experience every kind of pressure, we're not crushed. At times we don't know what to do, but quitting is not an option. We are

persecuted by others, but God has not forsaken us. We may be knocked down, but not out" (2 Cor 4:7-9 TPT). During all of this we are more than conquerors by the power of His love (Rom. 8:37). Even so, we need be aware that yielding to His work within us, sometimes means that there is a personal sacrifice involved.

Death that Leads to Life

We have been made alive with Christ and we are a new creation. God does not want to kill the new creation, but sometimes we need to die to our personal ambitions and the fleshly patterns of our old life.

"We continually share in the death of Jesus in our own bodies so that the resurrection life of Jesus will be revealed through our humanity. We consider living to mean that we are constantly being handed over to death for Jesus' sake so that the life of Jesus will be revealed through our humanity" (2 Cor. 4:7-11).

When we die to our own ambitions to respond to what the Father is doing, it always means life and breakthrough for other people. *"So, then, death is at work in us but it releases life in you"* (2 Cor. 4:12 TPT). We can find this principle all throughout the Bible. Jesus confirms this as well: *"Except a corn of wheat fall into the ground and die, it abideth alone: but if it die, it bringeth forth much fruit"* (John 12:24). When we share in the death of Jesus by giving up our self-interest to lay down our life for other people, we will see great fruit. This is how become vessels for honorable work that bears much fruit.

A Vessel for Honorable Work

"Therefore, if anyone cleanses himself from these things [which are dishonorable—disobedient, sinful], he will be a vessel for honor, sanctified [set apart for a special purpose and], useful to the Master,

prepared for every good work" (2 Tim. 2:21 AMP). We have already seen that we cannot transform ourselves, but here we read that if we cleanse ourselves, we will become a vessel of honor. This may look like a contradiction to us. We often assume that either God is doing all the work, or that He has left it all up to us. Both of these assumptions are wrong. Our Father is the one who cleanses us, but we can either cooperate with Him, or say no to His work within us. Believers have often tried to explain the mystery of God's sovereignty and our free will in two very opposite ways:

1. ***God is sovereign and does whatever He wants.***
    Within some parts of the body of Christ, there has been such a strong focus on the sovereignty of God that there is almost no place to respond at all. That creates passive believers who live limited lives. We are called to partner with Him to see his will released in this world.

2. ***Jesus has done His part, and the rest is up to us.***
    Others have focused so much on the believer's response to God that it almost seems like everything has been left up to us. The room for God's work becomes minimized, and Jesus becomes dependent upon our will and choice. That creates stressed out believers who don't know how to rest in Christ.

Since our transformation involves God's power and our free will, both assumptions are wrong. This is not an either–or situation. Our Father wants a dynamic relationship with His children. This means that at times, He initiates and we get to respond to Him. At other times, we take the initiative and He responds to us. We are called to partner with Jesus Christ so that His will can break through in this world.

We are Called to Partner with Jesus

This becomes clear once we understand that we have synergistic relationship with God, meaning that both His will and our will is important. God has not created the world in such a way that He is in control of everything that happens. Every created being has an amount of free will, especially human beings. This is the reason our choice is important. For His will to be accomplished in our lives, we need to cooperate with what He is doing. In this way, we are partnering with Jesus so that His will can be done in this world. As we continue to respond to His love, we become a vessel for His love and we will bear fruit in the Kingdom of God. There are several things that we can do to release the will of God on the earth, and I will expand on some of them throughout this book. Here I just want to list a few examples as an illustration of the dynamics of how we are to partner with God to release His will:

- Prayer and intercession
- Preaching the gospel
- Fasting
- Fulfilling our God given dreams and visions
- Worship
- Stewarding our gifts

This has nothing to do with walking in legalism or trying to make the Kingdom of God come in our own strength. It simply means abiding in the love of God and responding to His will. When we do that, His power and grace can operate through us. This is an amazing privilege!

God Initiates, We Respond

"Now you must continue to make this new life fully manifested as you live in the holy awe of God—which brings you trembling into his

presence. God will continually revitalize you, implanting within you the passion to do what pleases him" (Phil. 2:12-13 TPT).

For two persons to build a meaningful relationship, it always requires that both parts invest time, attention and effort together. The same is true in our relationship with God. He is the one who has the initiative, but our response is important as well. Abiding in the love of the Father doesn't mean that we are to stay passive, but to respond so that His will can be accomplished in us. We're yielding to what He is doing by giving Him access to the areas of our lives that need transformation. Investing in our relationship with God by giving time, money and attention is how we build a dynamic life together with Him. Life with God becomes boring if we remain passive and just wait on Him all the time.

Waiting on God does not Equal Passivity

The Bible has a lot to say when it comes to waiting on God. Here is one example: *"But those who wait on the Lord Shall renew their strength; They shall mount up with wings like eagles, They shall run and not be weary, They shall walk and not faint"* (Isa. 40:31 NKJV).
This is a wonderful promise about the renewal and refreshing that we receive by waiting on the Lord. All of us should learn to wait on the Lord, but at the same time we need to understand that waiting on the Lord is not the same as being passive. To wait on God means to spend time in His presence, yielding to Him by abiding in His Words and walking in the Spirit. One of the ways to do that is by developing good habits. The habits in themselves will not transform us, but by developing such habits we give the Holy Spirit space to continue His transforming work in our lives.

CHAPTER 2: THE POWER OF GOOD HABITS

On the other hand, discipline yourself for the purpose of godliness [keeping yourself spiritually fit]. For physical training is of some value, but godliness (spiritual training) is of value in everything and in every way, since it holds promise for the present life and for the life to come (1 Tim. 4:7-9 AMP).

Learning to yield to the work of the Holy Spirit is connected to spiritual disciplines. To build spiritual disciplines as a training in godliness is always a long-term work, and we are empowered by the grace of God to take small steps in the right direction. My life is an example of this. I had to take a journey with Jesus that killed my spiritual ambitions. During this journey, I learned to value a much more measured approach to my life with God. When Jesus came into my life, prayer and mission became very important to me. I loved to read biographies of men and women of God from church history, who had devoted their life to God through prayer and missions.

This was a very formative time for me. It stirred a deep hunger and passion in me for the things of God, which is still burning in me to today. Some of these books are still among my favorites. I go back to read them every now and then to stir up the revelation and fire that these books bring. Since they tell the life stories of people who lived very radical lives and prayed for hours every day, I thought that I had to imitate them to live close to God.

My problem was that I was nowhere near their level of spiritual maturity, and neither did I have the insight into the heart of the Father and the New Covenant that I have now. Because of this, I ended up with a legalistic approach to my life with the Father. It was only after my spiritual burnout, the one which I wrote about in the introduction of this book, that I started to build healthier habits that I could keep practicing over time. One of the lessons that I learned through that season is that nothing can quench our longing for a more intimate life with the Father like legalism and religious pressure.

Small and Realistic Steps

Suffer hardship with me, as a good soldier of Christ Jesus. No soldier in active service entangles himself in the affairs of everyday life, so that he may please the one who enlisted him. And if someone likewise competes as an athlete, he is not crowned as victor unless he competes according to the rules. The hard-working farmer ought to be the first to receive his share of the crops (2 Tim. 2:3-6 NASB).

Paul is the apostle of grace. Yet, he has a lot to say about spiritual disciplines. He uses the pictures of a soldier, an athlete and a very hard-working farmer to describe the type of focus and discipline that we need as believers. No one will become a top-level athlete overnight, and neither is it possible to become a soldier without lots of preparation. The same applies to us as believers. Building good habits and spiritual disciplines by taking small steps in the right direction will cause us to grow strong in spirit. Good habits have a lot in common with eating. To prepare food and to eat a couple of meals every day is an ordinary part of life, and it does not feel like such a big deal to most of us. Still, these repeated meals will keep us healthy and well nurtured. The same is true when it comes to spiritual disciplines that build our life with God. They keep our inner man healthy and strong.

When you find a good way of reading the Bible and praying that works for you, and you stay consistent with it, your spiritual life will stay healthy. For example, being committed to reading the Bible and praying for twenty minutes a day might not sound like much. But by keeping on doing that, we continue to get a steady dose of the Word of God into our spirit every day, and the impact will be powerful. The length of our prayers or how much we read in the Bible is not the most important thing. Our focus should be to get nourished by the Word and the Spirit. It is all about staying connected to God and learning to abide in His love.

Being Satisfied & Fulfilled in the Spirit

So how much should we pray and read the Bible every day? The answer is simple: Eat the Word of God and spend time with Jesus until your spirit is satisfied. There are no set measures for how much we should read our Bible and pray. Neither has God given any specific instruction on when to do it. The important thing is that we find a flow in our relationship with the Father where our hearts are satisfied by His love. Again, this has a lot in common with eating. We eat until we are full and satisfied. In the same way, we keep eating the Word and drinking the presence of the Holy Spirit until we are fully satisfied.

Spiritual Disciplines Were Given for Our Sake

Jesus made a short statement that reveals an important principle concerning spiritual disciplines when He said: *"The Sabbath was made for man, and not man for the sabbath: therefore the Son of man is Lord also of the Sabbath" (Mark. 2:27-28).* God gave the Sabbath for our sake; He did not create us to keep the Sabbath. This is true about all spiritual disciplines. They are given to help us build the secret place with the Father. Our goal must always be to know Him more. If spiritual disciplines help us to reach that goal, they are a blessing. But if we lose sight of the real goal by making spiritual disciplines a goal within themselves, they have lost their purpose. When that happen, they will become a distraction and if they do, we need do find new and fresh ways of spending time with our heavenly Father. The point is finding nourishment and food for our spirit by fellowshipping with Him. That is the only way we can find true contentment and fulfilment with Jesus.

Seeing the Greatness of Small Beginnings

We should never underestimate the power of taking small steps in the right direction. The prophet Zechariah pointed to this truth through his prophetic preaching. One of the major points of the book of Zechariah is that we need to learn to see the greatness in small beginnings. Zechariah partnered with the prophet Haggai to strengthen the people of God in their work of restoring the city of Jerusalem and the temple. The work of restoration had been hindered because of pressure from the enemies of Israel, but the leaders and the people of Israel found new strength through the ministry of these young prophets (See Ezra 4:1-6:18).

Zechariah made a prophetic declaration concerning the success of their work on the restoration of the temple when he said: *"The hands of Zerubbabel have laid the foundation of this temple; His hands shall also finish it. Then you will know that the Lord of hosts has sent me to you. For who has despised the day of small things"* (Zech. 4:9-10 NKJV)? Just like the rebuilding of the temple in Jerusalem started in a small and unspectacular way, so it is in our lives when we are developing good habits. We might start by taking small steps, and it is easy to dismiss these as being insignificant. But we need to learn how to see the greatness in that which is small. This is how the Kingdom of God is extended.

Understanding How the Kingdom of God is Growing

Jesus said that the *"… kingdom of heaven is like a mustard seed, which a man took and sowed in his field, which indeed is the least of all the seeds; but when it is grown it is greater than the herbs and becomes a tree, so that the birds of the air come and nest in its branches"* (Matt. 13:31-32 NKJV). When the Kingdom of God is planted within us, it is usually planted as a small seed, but it grows until it becomes bigger than all the other trees. I believe that this is a good way of describing how the habits we develop can transform our lives. Developing a daily habit of praying and reading the Bible is like a small seed of the Kingdom being planted within our hearts. But that seed will grow into a big tree, from which we will be able to eat the sweet fruit of intimacy with God.

Good habits become a highway, through which the Father's love can permeate our whole being. Jesus described that the Kingdom of God *"…is like unto leaven, which a woman took, and hid in three measures of meal, till the whole was leavened"* (Matt. 13:33). The Kingdom of God is planted as a tiny seed, but as we nurture the seed by staying connected to Jesus, it starts to grow and permeate us until every area of our inner life has been transformed by the love of God. Small priorities can bring about great results.

As I look back at my life, it has not been the powerful encounters that has impacted me the most. Rather it has been the daily habits of praying, reading the Bible and building a lifestyle of worship. As we have already seen, spiritual disciplines can't transform us, but they give the Holy Spirit something to work with in our lives. We see this clearly illustrated by another example from the Old Testament.

The Example of Daniel

"But when Daniel learned that the law had been signed, he went home and knelt down as usual in his upstairs room, with its windows open toward Jerusalem. He prayed three times a day, just as he had always done, giving thanks to his God." (Dan. 6:10 NLT). Daniel structured his life around the habit of praying three times a day, which he did in a room where he could pray toward Jerusalem. This shows us that he looked in the direction of God's promises while he was praying. Jerusalem was the center of the promised land, where

the temple was built, and where all the feasts were celebrated. Jerusalem represented the inheritance of the people of God. Even though they lived in exile at the time, Daniel centered his life in prayer around the promise of freedom and future return to their promised land. Daniel prayed three times a day, but because he was one of the most prominent men in Babylon, we can assume that he was a very busy man (Dan. 2:48-49). It is unlikely that he would have had the time to pray for hours at a time, but he was consistent in praying three times a day. Daniel also combined a life of prayer with periods of fasting (Dan. 1:8-16, 9:1-3). Because of this, Daniel had developed a deep relationship with God and his life was surrounded by the favor and protection of the Father.

Daniel and Prophetic Intercession

Daniel cultivated a prayer life that became so deep and rich that when it was time for the Jewish people to be delivered from exile, he partnered with God through intercessory prayer to help bring about their deliverance. Even though Daniel was a busy man holding a prominent position in the government, he kept his awareness of the prophetic timing of heaven. He says that *"... I Daniel understood by books the number of the years, whereof the word of the LORD came to Jeremiah the prophet, that he would accomplish seventy years in the desolations of Jerusalem"* (Dan. 9:2). It was not just Daniel's awareness of God's prophetic timing that reveals his character, but his response reveals his heart even more: *"And I set my face unto the Lord God, to seek by prayer and supplications, with fasting, and sackcloth, and ashes"* (Dan. 9:3). Daniel did not just sit and wait for the prophetic promises to be fulfilled. His heart had been so merged with the heart of God, that the burden to see the will of God accomplished was so strong that he needed to respond. Therefore, Daniel gave himself to prayer and fasting for the prophetic words spoken by Jeremiah to come to pass.

Through intercession, Daniel co-labored with God to release his promises into the earth. Living in a lifestyle of prayer helped him to develop a deep connection to the heart of God, so that he could discern the times and seasons of heaven. Another result of his prayer life was that Daniel walked in high levels of revelation that gave him insight into the counsel of God. Numerous times he received angelic visitations that provided prophetic insight into God's plan of salvation and the coming Messiah. All of this started with a small commitment to prayer. Daniel's testimony is an inspiration for all of us to develop good habits that we practice faithfully. Powerful things happen when we take small steps to develop intimacy with God.

CHAPTER 3: THE REWARD OF THE SECRET PLACE

"But when you give to the needy, do not let your left hand know what your right hand is doing, so that your giving may be in secret. Then your Father, who sees what is done in secret, will reward you" (Matt. 6:3-4 NIV).

"But when you pray, go into your room, close the door and pray to your Father, who is unseen. Then your Father, who sees what is done in secret, will reward you" (Matt. 6:6 NIV).

"But when you fast, put oil on your head and wash your face, so that it will not be obvious to others that you are fasting, but only to your Father, who is unseen; and your Father, who sees what is done in secret, will reward you" (Matt. 6:17-18 NIV).

In the sermon on the mount, Jesus is encouraging us to build our relationship with the Father by investing into the secret place. When I use the term *"the secret place"*, I'm referring to our hidden relationship with God. It is in the secret place that we get to know His heart and it is there we learn to abide in His love. Jesus uses giving, praying and fasting as examples of how we can invest in our relationship with the Father who always rewards those who live for His eyes only. Notice how Jesus keeps pointing to the Father in these passages. His desire is for us to develop a life of intimacy with the Father, knowing that when we do things from of a heart of sonship, He sees it and will respond.

The Secret Place of the Heart

The secret place is not a physical room, even though some people prefer to have a certain room dedicated for prayer and devotion.

The secret place is the chamber in our heart where we encounter God. This means that we carry the secret place with us wherever we go, so that we can stay connected to God's heart all the time. Whether we are working or traveling somewhere, or even while we spend time with friends and family, we can stay connected to the heart of the Father. Our place of fellowship and intimacy with Him is within us.

This has been a big blessing for me. Since I am traveling a lot, I'm spending a huge amount of time on airplanes, trains and busses. That time has now become times of encounter and revelation for me. Traveling by train or airplane is a great time to soak in His presence, meditate on scripture, or listen to an anointed teaching. I am never alone because God is always with me and He is the best and most faithful friend there is. It is precious to the Father when we make choices to prioritize our relationship with Him. God is always looking for reasons to reward us when we do that. He is a generous Father and giving rewards is part of His nature.

God is a Rewarder

Our Father loves to reward His children, especially when we are seeking Him diligently. Generosity is one of His most prominent character traits. The book of Hebrews says that *"…without faith it is impossible to please him: for he that cometh to God must believe that he is, and that he is a rewarder of them that diligently seek him"* (Hebr. 11:6). Sometimes, the fear of becoming performance-based in our relationship with God has caused us to be a little cautious to talk about heavenly rewards. If thinking of the Father rewarding us causes you to be afraid, there is no need to worry. God is not measuring your performance to find out if you are doing enough good deeds for Him to bless you. That is not what these texts are about at all. We need to realize that the Father is so generous that He tries to find every way possible to encourage and reward His kids. He always rewards us based on His kindness and grace.

Sometimes the fear of legalism creates a passive way of relating to God. Since He is a rewarder of those who diligently seek Him, passivity can cause us to miss out on the blessings He wants to give to us. We should be aware of the trap of legalism, but at the same time we need to remember that the answer to legalism is to know God's loving and generous heart. In that way, we can walk in a bold relationship with Him that is full of joy, while knowing that He always rewards by grace alone.

The Father's Reward System Operates by Grace

This is the point of the parable about the workers in the vineyard. Jesus shared this story when He was teaching on this very subject (Matt. 20:1-16). The owner of this vineyard needed more laborers to come and work in the vineyard, so he went out to hire people for that purpose at different times during the day. Some workers worked in the vineyard all day, while other workers were hired a few hours later. Some were hired at lunch time and still others in the afternoon. Some of them even worked for only one hour of the day. This last group were people who no one else wanted to hire, but our Father loves to work with this group. He chooses the workers whom others have rejected (Matt. 20:6-7). This is the reason they were hired to come and work in the vineyard.

These different groups of workers were hired at different hours of the day, and they didn't work the same amount of time. Yet, they all received the exact same salary. This seemed unfair to the ones that had been working all day, enduring the heat and the heavy workload. So, they went to the owner of the vineyard to complain about this issue:

"Those people worked only one hour, and yet you've paid them just as much as you paid us who worked all day in the scorching heat.' "He answered one of them, 'Friend, I haven't been unfair! Didn't you agree to work all day for the usual wage? Take your money and go. I wanted

to pay this last worker the same as you. Is it against the law for me to do what I want with my money? Should you be jealous because I am kind to others?' "So those who are last now will be first then, and those who are first will be last" (Matt. 20:12-16 NLT).

They became jealous because of the kindness of their employer. Like so many of Jesus' teachings, this parable is meant to be a bit provoking. It strikes at the heart of performance-based religion. Because we have read this parable so many times, it is sometimes easy to get a little too familiar with it. But if we put ourselves in the places of these hired workers, most of us would be upset if we worked for a boss who paid his employers out of the kindness of his heart. Imagine yourself working for a boss who would pay the same salary to all his employers, regardless of if they are working full time, half time, or maybe even only for a few hours a week. Any boss who would run his company like that would end up in bankruptcy fast, but the Kingdom of God doesn't work like a worldly company. It is the Father's house and our Father has unlimited riches. Jesus rules His kingdom in humility and grace, which means that the rewards that He gives will never be based on our performance, but always on His grace alone.

Expect to be Rewarded Abundantly

Knowing that God responds by rewarding me when I make the active choices to develop my life with Him is such an inspiration. He loves to shower us with generous gifts and heavenly rewards. Because His system of reward operates by grace, I come boldly to Him in prayer, expecting the answers to my prayers to be even better than I thought. Being aware of the reward ahead of him, gave Moses the strength he needed to endure the hardships of leading the people of Israel out of Egypt. The writer of Hebrews tells us concerning Moses that *"He thought it was better to suffer for the sake of Christ than to own the treasures of Egypt, for he was looking ahead to his great reward"* (Hebr. 11:26 NLT). Wanting the reward is a legitimate reason for a life of prayer and obedience. When I invest in my relationship with the Father, I have come to expect to be rewarded abundantly, just because He loves me so much. God is the giver of good gifts!

God Gives Good Gifts

We started this chapter by reading a couple of verses from the sermon on the mount. A little later in that same sermon, Jesus makes the following statement:

Ask and keep on asking and it will be given to you; seek and keep on seeking and you will find; knock and keep on knocking and the door will be opened to you. For everyone who keeps on asking receives, and he who keeps on seeking finds, and to him who keeps on knocking, it will be opened… how much more will your Father who is in heaven [perfect as He is] give what is good and advantageous to those who keep on asking Him (Matt. 7:7-8, 11 AMP).

Jesus tells us to do three things to build a dynamic life with God. When we do these three things, we step into an exciting lifestyle of heavenly provision. These three things are:

1. *Ask and keep on asking,* and it will be given to you.
2. *Seek and keep on seeking,* and you will find.
3. *Knock and keep on knocking,* and the door will open.

We have a very good Father who loves to give generous and perfect gifts to those who ask Him for it. Again, it is important to remember that He is not measuring our performance to find out if we have earned them. Instead, God is looking for reasons to reward us. This is the reason why Jesus encourages us to invest in our relationship with the Father. Because He is good, He only has good and perfect gifts to give: *"Do not be deceived, my beloved brethren. Every good gift and every perfect gift is from above, and comes down from the Father of lights, with whom there is no variation or shadow of turning"* (Jam. 1:16-17 NKJV).

The Grace of God & The Judgement Seat of Christ

It is by considering the parable of the workers in the vineyard that we can understand the judgement seat of Christ and how He will reward our deeds. There will come a day when all of us will stand before Jesus to receive our heavenly reward.

For we must all appear before the judgment seat of Christ, so that each one may receive compensation for his deeds done through the body, in accordance with what he has done, whether good or bad (2 Cor. 5:10 NASB).

Scriptures like this one has sometimes been interpreted in very legalistic ways, which has caused a lot of anxiety. This has been done by believers who lack understanding of how the Kingdom of God operates. We need to understand that the judgement seat of Christ is the throne of grace, where we come to receive mercy and grace in time of need. As we have already seen, the heavenly reward system operates by grace. God rewards us because He is a good and generous Father. The sins and the transgressions we have committed, as well as all our personal failures have already been reconciled and forgiven through the finished work of Jesus Christ (1 John 2:1-2). Since they have already been dealt with on the cross, our sins and evil deeds will never be punished again. If God were to punish our sins again, He would be unjust since our sins has already been wiped out. The Father no longer holds our sins against us and Jesus is actively looking for new ways to reward us!

Receiving Our Praise from God

This is what Paul is expressing in one of his letters to the church in Corinth: *"Therefore do not go on passing judgment before the time, but wait until the Lord comes, who will both bring to light the things hidden in the darkness and disclose the motives of human hearts; and then praise will come to each person from God"(1 Cor. 4:5 NASB).* As the hidden things and our motives are brought into the light, that will not be done to condemn us, shame us, or even to tell us what a mess we made of life. When Jesus unveils the hidden parts of our lives and our motives, we will receive our praise from Him. It basically means that Jesus will tell us: *"Well done, thou good and faithful servant: thou hast been faithful over a few things, I will make thee ruler over many things: enter thou into the joy of thy lord" (Matt. 25:21).* We are then going to receive our praise and our heavenly rewards from our Savior and friend, Jesus Christ.

Rewarded Because of What Jesus Is Doing through Us

Now we have finally arrived at the great unveiling of how gracious and brilliant God's heavenly system of rewards really is. When you stand before the judgement seat of Christ, you will be rewarded *for what Jesus has accomplished through you!* We are not rewarded based on our own good works, but because of how the life of Jesus Christ has manifested through us. Christ in us is our hope of glory (Col. 1:27).

Paul writes that we need to make sure that we are building on the right foundation. *"But let each one take heed how he builds on it. For no other foundation can anyone lay than that which is laid, which is Jesus Christ. Now if anyone builds on this foundation with gold, silver, precious stones, wood, hay, straw…" (1 Cor. 3:10-12 NKJV).* The only foundation that we can build on is that of Jesus Christ Himself. So, how can we build with gold, silver, and precious stones? We can't do that by ourselves, but Jesus can and He lives within us. *"I have been crucified with Christ; it is no longer I who live, but Christ lives in me; and the life which I now live in the flesh I live by faith in the Son of God, who loved me and gave Himself for me"* (Gal. 2:20 NKJV). As we learn to partner with Jesus Christ, He will live His life through us and that will produce the gold, silver and precious stones. We will then walk in His character, which will cause us to be more than overcomers through Him who loves us (Rom. 8:37). This is how we receive the rewards of heaven. Jesus rewards us for what He is doing through us. As we surrender to Him and partner with His love that is flowing through us, the blessings of heaven will manifest. When Paul continues to write, he states that: *"… each one's work will become clear; for the Day will declare it, because it will be revealed by fire; and the fire will test each one's work, of what sort it is. If anyone's work which he has built on it endures, he will receive a reward"* (1 Cor. 3:13 NKJV). The only work that endures is that which Jesus has accomplished through us, which means that we will be rewarded by partnering with Him so that we reveal His life. This is good news!

Who is Rewarded?

As Jesus lives His life through us, that will lead to a lifestyle that the Father rewards. We have already seen that the reward system of heaven operates by grace alone, meaning that He rewards us because He is good and generous to us. We do not earn it, but we receive it based only on what His grace accomplishes through us. By partnering with His grace, our lives are transformed to reflect Jesus Christ and that is what God wants. Below I have listed the characteristics of a lifestyle that God rewards. The people who will receive His rewards are the ones that:

- **Invest in the secret place.** Jesus only did what He saw the Father doing and as we surrender to His indwelling life, we will also live to please our Father (John 5:19). We have already seen how the Father rewards the one who invests in his or her relationship with Him in the secret place. The Father honors the people who invest time to know Him in a deeper way. *"But when you pray, go into your room, close the door and pray to your Father, who is unseen. Then your Father, who sees what is done in secret, will reward you"* (Matt. 6:6 NIV see also Matt 6:3-4, 17-18).

- **Walk in humility.** The nature of Jesus is humility and as we allow Him to transform our lives, we will walk in humility as well (Phil. 2:8-11). Our Father loves a humble heart and He always honors and rewards those who walk in humility. The humble person will be exalted and receive a reward of honor, riches and life. *"By humility and the fear of the Lord are riches, and honour, and life"* (Prov. 22:4). *"Humble yourselves therefore under the mighty hand of God, that he may exalt you in due time"* (1 Pet. 5:6, Jam. 4:10).

- **Serve the Lord faithfully and wholeheartedly.** Jesus lived to reveal and glorify the Father and He did that faithfully all His life (John 17:4). As we allow Jesus to live through us, our focus will also be to live according to the Father's will. He does not reward us according to the visible results of our work or how big our ministry and influence is. He rewards us according to our faithfulness to His calling and our motivation to serve Him alone. He does not look at our numbers, but at the motivation of our heart. This is important to remember. Otherwise, we could easily become discouraged by the lack of results of our work, or we will end up in pride because of the fruit we produce. *"And whatsoever ye do, do it heartily, as to the Lord, and not unto men; Knowing that of the Lord ye shall receive the reward of the inheritance: for ye serve the Lord Christ"* (Col. 3:22-23 see also 1 Cor. 15:58 and Matt. 25:21).

- **Overcome.** Jesus has overcome the world and because He indwells us, we overcome together with Him. We have been given a lot of promises of being rewarded for being overcomers. This is not something that we strive to do, but as children of God, we are overcomers (1 John 2:13-14, 5:4-5). By walking in our identity as overcomers we will overcome sin, the world, and the devil to rule and reign with Christ forever. *"To him that overcometh will I grant to sit with me in my throne, even as I also overcame, and am set down with my Father in his throne"* (Rev. 3:21 see also Rev. 2:7, 11, 17, 26, 3:5, 12, 21:7 and 2 Tim. 4:7-8).

- **Overcome temptation.** Jesus overcame all the devil's temptations and, He will overcome through us as well if we allow Him. Life is full of temptations and suffering. These tend to make us or break us, but as we abide in the love of the Father there is grace to overcome and stay faithful to Him. We will be richly rewarded for doing so. *"Blessed is the man that endureth temptation: for when he is tried, he shall receive the crown of life, which the Lord hath promised to them that love him"* (Jam. 1:12).

- **Overcome deception.** Jesus is the truth and as we abide in Him, we will keep on walking in truth as well. There is a lot of deception in the world today and we will come across deceptive doctrines and ideas. As we overcome deception by through love of the Father and by walking in fellowship with Jesus, we will be richly rewarded by God. *"For many deceivers have gone out into the world, those who do not acknowledge Jesus Christ as coming in the flesh. This is the deceiver and the antichrist. Watch yourselves, that you do not lose what we have accomplished, but that you may receive a full reward"* (2 John 1:7-8 NASB).

- **Build on Jesus as the foundation.** Jesus is building His church and the gates of hell cannot stand against, nor can they overpower the church that Jesus is building (Matt. 16:17-19). Since Jesus indwells us, He is now building His church through us. When Paul writes that we will be rewarded according to whatever we have built on the foundation of Jesus Christ, this is what he means. Since Jesus Christ lives within us, we are rewarded according to what He has been allowed to accomplish through us, which is probably much more than we know. *"…every man's work shall be made manifest: for the day shall declare it, because it shall be revealed by fire; and the fire shall try every man's work of what sort it is. If any man's work abide which he hath built thereupon, he shall receive a reward (1 Cor. 3:12-14).*

- **Receive and honor the servants of God.** Jesus indwells us, but He also ministers to us through His body. There is a reward from heaven for us when we receive from the people that God has raised up and anointed to serve us. When we do that, we receive an impartation from the anointing upon their life which basically means that we receive more of Jesus Himself. *"He that receiveth a prophet in the name of a prophet shall receive a prophet's reward; and he that receiveth a righteous man in the name of a righteous man shall receive a righteous man's reward"* (Matt. 10:41 *see also Luke 10:16*).

- **Honor and serve the children of God.** Just like Jesus washed the feet of His disciples in the gospel of John, He keeps on doing that today (John 13:5-20). But now He is doing it through us. As we honor and serve our fellow believers, we will be rewarded by our heavenly Father. By loving His children, we are honoring and delighting His heart. There is a reward for loving and serving the family of God. *"And whosoever shall give to drink unto one of these little ones a cup of cold water only in the name of a disciple, verily I say unto you, he shall in no wise lose his reward"* (Matt. 10:42 see also Mark 9:41 and Gal. 6:8-10).

- **Sacrifice for Jesus.** Jesus sacrificed everything to bring us home to the Father. As His life shapes ours, sacrificing to reach people with the love of the Father becomes our lifestyle. At times, there will be sacrifices as we walk with God and sometimes these sacrifices will be huge. The good news is that these sacrifices will not be greater than the rewards we will receive from heaven. Already in this life we are promised to receive hundredfold back. *"There is no man that hath left house, or brethren, or sisters, or father, or mother, or wife, or children, or lands, for my sake, and the gospel's, but he shall receive an hundredfold now in this time, houses, and brethren, and sisters, and mothers, and children, and lands, with persecutions; and in the world to come eternal life"* (Mark 10:29-30).

This list reveals the type of lifestyle that God rewards, but as you probably noticed, all these characteristics are part of who Jesus is. He is humble, faithful and the One who builds of the Kingdom of God. This reveal how gracious and brilliant the reward system of heaven really is. Heavenly rewards are not about what we do for God. *It is all about allowing the life of Christ to flow through us!*

What Is the Reward?

We have been studying about the heavenly rewards throughout this chapter. We have seen how the Father gives them, but what are these rewards? The Bible uses a couple of different pictures to describe them, for example the crown of righteousness and the crown of life (Jam. 1:12, Rev. 2:10). These are descriptions of our royal inheritance as children of God that manifests because we are partnering with Jesus. Our Father rewards us in many ways, but the ultimate reward is to know God and develop friendship with Him.

The Lord gave this promise to Abraham: *"After these things the word of the Lord came to Abram in a vision, saying, "Do not be afraid, Abram. I am your shield, your exceedingly great reward"* (Gen. 15:1 NKJV). A life in intimacy with God brings great rewards, but that is not the most important thing. The ultimate reward for building the secret place with the Father is a deeper revelation of His love. When we seek Him, we will find Him, which will compel us to seek Him more and then we will find Him again. Deep will cry out too deep as we go on a glorious journey into His heart (Ps. 42:7-8). By growing in intimacy with Him, we store our treasures in heaven and set our heart in the right direction.

Where Our Treasure Is Our Heart Will Be

We started this chapter by studying how Jesus encourages us to invest in the secret place. A few sentences later, Jesus explains why we are to do that by making the following point: *"But store up for yourselves treasures in heaven, where moths and vermin do not destroy, and where thieves do not break in and steal. For where your treasure is, there your heart will be also"* (Matt. 6:20-21 NIV). Jesus tells us to store up our treasures in heaven. When we follow His advice, our heart will be set in the direction of the Kingdom of God, which means that our attention will naturally be focused on our relationship with the Father. Over time, we will develop a lifestyle where our heart is in constant connection with Him. Our inner life and desires will then be aligned with His. This is the way Jesus lived, and this is how He could do what the Father was doing (Joh. 5:19). The reward of building a life in the secret place is to have a connection with the heart of God that reveals Jesus to the world. It is with this in mind that we will start to look at specific spiritual disciplines. But first we need to look at our motivation. Jesus is always after what's in our heart. He doesn't want just our good deeds, but He wants to possess our heart with His love. That is the difference between a life in bondage or a life in freedom.

CHAPTER 4: MOTIVATED BY LOVE

There have been a lot of religious teachings connected to spiritual disciplines and building the secret place with God. As a result of that, a lot of people have confused building habits to strengthen our relationship with the Father with religious performance. It is important to realize that being disciplined has nothing to do with earning the blessings or approval of God.

Look with wonder at the depth of the Father's marvelous love that he has lavished on us! He has called us and made us his very own beloved children. The reason the world doesn't recognize who we are is that they didn't recognize him. Beloved, we are God's children right now (1 John 3:1-2 TPT).

We are always unconditionally loved by our heavenly Father. He is always well pleased with us. That revelation needs to be at the foundation of everything that our lives is built upon.

Four Important Truths to Remember

As we abide in His love, our hearts are transformed and that will result in a new lifestyle. This happens as we get a deeper insight into who Jesus is and by knowing Him. The fruit of seeing Him as He truly is, will always be a growing desire for purity within our hearts: *"… however, it is not yet apparent what we will become. But we do know that when it is finally made visible, we will be just like him, for we will see him as he truly is. And all who focus their hope on him will always be purifying themselves, just as Jesus is pure"* (1 John 3:2-3 TPT). Notice that all transformation is based on a revelation of Jesus Christ. Spiritual disciplines are means through which we can live out our revelation express our love for the Father, so that freedom can grow in our lives. To understand the role of spiritual disciplines from a biblical perspective, there are four important truths to remember:

1. **Spiritual disciplines do not change God.**
    We are not practicing spiritual disciplines to change God or cause Him to give us more blessings. *"Jesus Christ the same yesterday, and today, and forever" (Hebr. 13:8).* Our Father has already blessed us with all spiritual blessings in heavenly places in Christ (Eph. 1:3). We have already received our full inheritance, being made coheirs with Him (Rom. 8:17). We are His children and the Kingdom of God belongs to us. Spiritual disciplines add nothing to our inheritance in Christ, and it doesn't cause God to love us more. He loves us perfectly already, and His love is both eternal and unchangeable.

2. **Spiritual disciplines do not change our identity.**
    Another important truth is that our identity as children of God never changes. Our value is not upgraded if we excel in spiritual disciplines, and neither are we losing our value to the Father if we fail. Jesus provided a new identity for us through the cross. We did nothing to earn our identity and we cannot do anything to ruin it either. Our identity is always stable and secure because we are in Christ. We will always be our Father's beloved and favored children, no matter what happens in our lives.

3. **Spiritual disciplines transform us.**
    The person who is transformed by practicing spiritual disciplines is you and me. We become sensitive to God when we focus on Him. Our spiritual hunger increases so that we can receive a fresh anointing and live out the blessings that we have received in Christ. By practicing spiritual disciplines, our focus will increase so that we can hear the voice of God more clearly.

4. **Spiritual disciplines help us to live according to our identity in Christ.** Spiritual disciplines will not give us a better identity before God but practicing them will help us to live according to who we are. As we have already seen, our value in His eyes will not increase or decrease based on our behavior. Our choices will affect our ability to live out our identity in Christ. For this reason, spiritual disciplines are important. They become a tool that the Holy Spirit is using to transform us into mature children.

Wrong Motivations for Practicing Spiritual Disciplines

When Jesus is teaching, He is always focusing on the motivation of the heart. His teachings are meant to reveal what compels and motivates us, so that we can surrender to Him and grow in love. His teaching on spiritual disciplines illustrates this in a perfect way. We find an example of this in the sermon on the mount. These passages are well-known to us. We studied them in the last chapter, but we are going to look at them again. This time from a different angle and a different translation:

Be especially careful when you are trying to be good so that you don't make a performance out of it. It might be good theater, but the God who made you won't be applauding. "When you do something for someone else, don't call attention to yourself" (Matt. 6:1 The Message).

Jesus instructs us to not do things to show our level of spirituality to other people. For the most part, our devotional life should be between us and God. Our Father wants laid down lovers, not play actors and performers. *"You've seen them in action, I'm sure — 'playactors' I call them — treating prayer meeting and street corner alike as a stage, acting compassionate as long as someone is watching, playing to the crowds. They get applause, true, but that's all they get…" (Matt. 6:2 The Message).*

Secrecy Is Not the Point, Our Motivation Is

There is no point in keeping things secret for the sake of secrecy, however. I used to be very religious about this topic. When I read about how Jesus wanted us to pray and give in secret, I thought that if anyone were to find out what I gave to God, the gift would lose its value. That is not what Jesus is saying. He said that we should not do things to be seen by men but doing them to be seen only by our Father. If people are asking about our devotional life, we are not missing out on anything by giving them an honest answer. It might even inspire them to take new steps to build a deeper relationship with the Father. At times, we must share our experiences and how we build our relationship with God, to help people and give them guidance.

Jesus is after our motivation. He wants us to practice spiritual disciplines like giving, prayer and fasting with the motivation of knowing Him and to grow in love for God and people. It is good to check our motives every now and then, especially since we are living in the era of social media, where we can share everything with the whole world all the time. *"And when you come before God, don't turn that into a theatrical production either. All these people making a regular show out of their prayers, hoping for fifteen minutes of fame! Do you think God sits in a box seat?"* (Matt. 6:5 The Message).

Trying to Earn Extra Favor with the Father

Another bad idea is to practice spiritual disciplines to gain extra favor with the Father. Jesus addressed this when He spoke to a self-righteous group of religious leaders. He shared the parable about the Pharisee and the tax collector with these leaders:

Two men went up to the temple to pray, one a Pharisee and the other a tax collector. The Pharisee stood and prayed thus with himself, 'God, I thank You that I am not like other men—extortioners, unjust, adulterers, or even as this tax collector. I fast twice a week; I give tithes of all that I possess (Luke 18:10-12 NKJV).

The Pharisee practiced spiritual disciplines to earn a righteous standing before the Father. If this is our motivation, we will not benefit from it at all. We will fall into pride and *"Pride goeth before destruction, and an haughty spirit before a fall" (Prov 16:18).* Paul warned us about how knowledge corrupts us if it is not received in humble love (1 Cor. 8:1-2). The Pharisee in this parable had lost his connection to God and he lacked spiritual discernment. Pride closes our hearts to God and shuts down spiritual vision.

The Importance of a Humble Heart

The tax collector humbled himself before God and because he did, he was the one who possessed true spiritual discernment. *"And the tax collector, standing afar off, would not so much as raise his eyes to heaven, but beat his breast, saying, 'God, be merciful to me a sinner!' (Luke 18:13 NKJV).* In his job as a tax collector, this man had been hired by Rome, who during that time occupied Israel. It was a huge betrayal, both against his own countrymen and the Jewish religion to work for the Roman Empire. On top of that, it was common practice among the tax collectors to demand more money than they were supposed to. They then took these money for themselves. Despite all this, and even though the tax collector seemed to be in a worse place than the Pharisee, he went home justified because He humbled himself before God. *"I tell you, this man went down to his house justified rather than the other; for everyone who exalts himself will be humbled, and he who humbles himself will be exalted" (Luke 18:14 NKJV).* Humility is always more important than good habits. Pride goes before a fall, but humility leads to exaltation from God.

Possessing a humble heart is more important than performing religious deeds because *"...God resisteth the proud, but giveth grace unto the humble"* (Jam. 4:6). Humility is the key that unlocks the greater depths of intimacy in our relationship with God. It is not bad to possess knowledge and be disciplined, but humility is the foundation for all spiritual growth. We never become experts in the things of God. Growing spiritually always means "growing down" to become like little children. This means losing prestige and our belief in our own competence in the things of God. We are all just little children with a big Father and we are totally and utterly dependent on Him. *"We sometimes tend to think we know all we need to know to answer these kinds of questions—but sometimes our humble hearts can help us more than our proud minds. We never really know enough until we recognize that God alone knows it all"* (1 Cor. 8:2-3 The Message).

The Example of Paul

Paul shares on the emptiness and futility of trying to serve God with wrong motives in Galatians, where he writes:

I tried keeping rules and working my head off to please God, and it didn't work. So I quit being a "law man" so that I could be God's man. Christ's life showed me how, and enabled me to do it. I identified myself completely with him. Indeed, I have been crucified with Christ (Gal. 2:19-20 The Message).

We can never please God by rule keeping, no matter how hard we try. This is the reason for which the law was given in the first place. It reveals that it is impossible to live up to God's standard. Only Jesus can live a righteous and holy life, and He wants to do it through us right now. Jesus indwells us and wants to live His life through us:

My ego is no longer central. It is no longer important that I appear righteous before you or have your good opinion, and I am no longer driven to impress God. Christ lives in me. The life you see me living is not "mine," but it is lived by faith in the Son of God, who loved me and gave himself for me. I am not going to go back on that (Gal. 2:20-21 The Message).

When we give up the hopeless task of trying to please God, and allow Jesus to take over, we are delivered from trying to impress God and appear spiritual before people. We can then serve them out of love and a pure heart. Being set free from the worry of our reputation and the struggle to keep up a good appearance is very liberating. This is an important part of our glorious freedom as the children of God. Our Father loves us, and He wants to give us all the approval and hugs that we will ever need!

Throughout the rest of this book, we will be studying specific spiritual disciplines, but it is important to remember the truths presented in this chapter. Let's make sure that we keep love as our motivation when building life in the secret place.

Part Two:

Spiritual Disciplines – Partnering with the Love of Christ

In this part of the book, we're going to study spiritual disciplines that can help us to partner with the love of Christ. To practice them is a way to respond to our desire for a deeper relationship with the Father. These are not laws to follow, but expressions of our desire to know His heart more. These spiritual disciplines are ways in which we partner with Jesus Christ so that His life can be formed in us. They have all been tremendous blessings for me. I hope that you will be inspired to deeper intimacy with God as we're studying these spiritual disciplines together!

CHAPTER 5: ENCOUNTERING JESUS THROUGH THE SCRIPTURES

In this chapter and the next, we will be looking at how we can respond to the love of the Father by encountering Jesus through the Scriptures. In the next chapter we will study our heart and its relation to the Word of God, but here we will start by looking at how the Scriptures reveal and impart the life of Jesus. Paul writes some powerful truths about the Bible here:

Remember what you were taught from your childhood from the Holy Scrolls which can impart to you wisdom to experience everlasting life through the faith of Jesus, the Anointed One! God has transmitted his very substance into every Scripture, for it is God-breathed. It will empower you by its instruction and correction, giving you the strength to take the right direction and lead you deeper into the path of godliness. Then you will be God's servant, fully mature and perfectly prepared to fulfill any assignment God gives you (2 Tim. 3:15-17 TPT).

The Bible is not an ordinary book. It is much more profound than writings of men who had experiences with God, and much more important than even any of the teachings of the great heroes of faith could ever be. The Bible is God-breathed and filled with His very substance. It is the Word of God. For us to grow in our relationship with God, it is vital that we are rooted and grounded in His Word.

As we read and abide in the words of Jesus Christ, we will find true freedom. Jesus said that *"If ye continue in my word, then are ye my disciples indeed; and ye shall know the truth, and the truth shall make you free" (John 8:31-32).* This is the only way to true freedom because as Jesus said a little later: *"If the Son therefore shall make you free, ye shall be free indeed" (John 8:36).* When we are reading the Bible, we are reading the words of Jesus Christ and by doing so we gain knowledge on spiritual matters. That is indeed a huge blessing, but we need to be aware that something much more important and profound happens. The words of Jesus impart His very own life and substance to us. Jesus said: *"It is the spirit that quickeneth; the flesh profiteth nothing: the words that I speak unto you, they are spirit, and they are life" (John 6:63).* When we read the Bible together with the Holy Spirit, we encounter Jesus Himself.

The Scriptures Point Us to Jesus

The Scriptures impart Spirit and Life because they testify about Jesus Christ. He is our life and by reading and meditating on the Scriptures we partake of Jesus Himself. *"You study the Scriptures diligently because you think that in them you have eternal life. These are the very Scriptures that testify about me, yet you refuse to come to me to have life" (John 5:39-40 NIV).* Therefore, when reading the Bible, we should always do it in fellowship with the Holy Spirit, allowing Him to bring revelation by unveiling Jesus through the Scriptures. The Bible is meant to point to Jesus, and to guide us into a deeper relationship with the Father. The goal of studying the Bible is to know the heart of the Father and experience more of Jesus.

This is the reason the scribes and Pharisees could not see who Jesus really was. They had a lot of knowledge but they lacked the revelation that only comes to us as the Holy Spirit illuminates the written Word. Their goal was to know the Scriptures, but they did not know the heart of God. Since they possessed knowledge without relationship, they were blind. Every promise within the Bible is an invitation to encounter the spiritual reality behind it. We can be deceived by relying on spiritual experiences, but if our Bible study does not lead to encounters with Jesus Christ and an impartation of the spiritual realities of which it speaks, we are deceived already. We need to know both the Scriptures and the power of God to walk in the Spirit.

Knowing the Scriptures & the Power of God

Several times during Jesus' ministry, the religious leaders sought to trap Jesus through theological debates and human arguments. During one of these occasions, the Sadducees challenged Jesus about His belief in the resurrection of the dead. Jesus reveals an important point through His answer: *"But Jesus answered and said to them, "You are mistaken, since you do not understand the Scriptures nor the power of God" (Matt. 22:29 NASB).* Jesus told them that they were mistaken, because they did not have revelation of the Word of God, but also because they did not know His power.

Our Father wants us to know and walk in the power of God, as well as knowing the Bible. Whenever we read a promise or see new things in the Scriptures, with that revelation always comes an invitation to encounter the spiritual reality of that promise. We should never settle for just seeing new things in the Bible, or to have a good understanding its message. The Word of God has only had its desired effect in our hearts when we are walking in the realities its truths. The good news is that His Word will not return empty, without first accomplishing that which it was sent to do.

The Word of God Will Not Return Empty

Since Jesus Christ is full of grace and truth, He always speaks forth the will of the Father and He cannot speak empty words. His Words will always be filled with His own life and substance, which is why Isaiah declares: *"So will My word be which goes out of My mouth; It will not return to Me empty, without accomplishing what I desire, and without succeeding in the purpose for which I sent it" (Isa. 55:11 NASB).* We can fully trust in the power of the Word of God. As we keep receiving His Words, they will never return empty. The Word of God is powerful and effective to accomplish everything that He intended it to do. It is beneficial to remember this when we read it.

Even though I sometimes feel uninspired while reading the Bible and even if I'm not getting big revelations every time I open it, I still know that the Word of God will not return void. Something always happen as I'm reading the Bible because this is not an ordinary book. The Word of God is living and powerful and it is working within our heart every time we read it. Even during the rest of the day and while we are asleep at night, His Word keeps working in our hearts until it has accomplished everything that the Father had intended.

Reading the Bible Together with the Holy Spirit

We need to remember that the New Testament was written by people who knew Jesus personally and had learned to abide in the love of the Father. If we want to understand the Word of God, we need to live in intimacy with Him as well. The Word always opens as we read it in fellowship with the Holy Spirit. In fact, it is only then that the Scriptures will impart life to us. We need the Holy Spirit to open the Word and enlighten the eyes of our hearts to see clearly. This is revealed in the prayer of Paul:

… the God of our Lord Jesus Christ, the Father of glory, may give unto you the spirit of wisdom and revelation in the knowledge of him: the eyes of your understanding being enlightened; that ye may know what is the hope of his calling, and what the riches of the glory of his inheritance in the saints, and what is the exceeding greatness of his power to us-ward who believe, according to the working of his mighty power (Eph. 1:17-19).

When we are reading the Bible while at the same time being enlightened by the Holy Spirit, three important things happen.

- We get a clear revelation of who Jesus is and everything He accomplished on the cross.
- We get deeper insight into the hope of our calling and the glory of our inheritance as sons and daughters.
- Another important benefit of reading the Bible together with the Holy Spirit is that the Scriptures are reading us, revealing what we have in our hearts.

The Word of God Pierces Our Heart

My experience of reading the Bible is that while I read the words within its pages, on a deeper level they are reading me, piercing my heart, and revealing my true motives. This helps me to live a transparent and honest life with God. In the book of Hebrews, we read the following: *"For the word of God is living and powerful, and sharper than any two-edged sword, piercing even to the division of soul and spirit, and of joints and marrow, and is a discerner of the thoughts and intents of the heart"* (Hebr. 4:12- 13 NKJV). The Word of God is so precise and sharp that it pierces through our whole being, dividing soul and spirit. It reveals our motives and it has power to transform our lives and heal our heart when we receive it in true humility. James writes: *"Therefore, ridding yourselves of all filthiness and all that remains of wickedness, in humility receive the word implanted, which is able to save your souls"* (Jam. 1:21 NASB). When we read and receive the Word of God with a humble heart, it restores and transforms our soul so that Jesus can be revealed even more through our lives.

Walking According to What We See

To receive the Word of God in humility means that we are to align our lives according to what we see in it. We are never told to walk in the Word, but to walk in the Spirit. We are called to walk according to the Word of God, by aligning our lives to what the Holy Spirit reveals within it. That is when the power of the Word of God is released through our lives: *"But prove yourselves doers of the word, and not just hearers who deceive themselves. For if anyone is a hearer of the word and not a doer, he is like a man who looks at his natural face in a mirror; for once he has looked at himself and gone away, he has immediately forgotten what kind of person he was"* (Jam. 1:23-24 NASB). We read the Bible to encounter Jesus Christ, but when we encounter Him, we see our true identity revealed. This happens because we are created in the image of Jesus Christ, and in Him our identity is revealed.

Walking according to what we see in the Word of God means to walk according to our identity as our Father's beloved kids. This is the reason James describes the Bible as our mirror. Within it, we see our true selves in Christ. But if we don't walk according to what we see there, we forget who we are and we will then live according to the false identities of broken humanity. When we're looking into the mirror of the Word of God and walk according to what we see, the Bible become a law of freedom that helps us walk in intimacy with the Father. *"But one who has looked intently at the perfect law, the law of freedom, and has continued in it, not having become a forgetful hearer but an active doer, this person will be blessed in what he does"* (Jam. 1:25 NASB).

The Bible Points to Its Author

The Bible is not a book of systematic theology, and neither does it give simple answers to the challenge of life. The Word of God points to its author, who possesses all knowledge concerning our lives. Jesus Himself wants to speak to us through every page of the Scriptures. As He does, we can draw near to Him by abiding in His Word. This is the reason for which the Bible was given to us. It points us to the Father and reveals His heart so that we can find our home in His presence. As we learn to abide in Him, we gain access to the answers and revelation that we need to prosper and be fruitful in our lives with Christ. This is what it means to walk in the Spirit.

A False Dichotomy

In certain parts of the body of Christ it has become very common to say that the Bible is not the word of God, but Jesus is. This may sound like a very Christ-centered statement, but it is a strange and false dichotomy. Of course, Jesus is the Word of God. The gospel of John states that clearly when speaking about Jesus: *"In the beginning was the Word, and the Word was with God, and the Word was God" (John 1:1).* Jesus is the Logos of God, but when Jesus is speaking about the Old Testament and how the religious leaders are reading it through their own traditions, He is saying that by doing so, they are *"…making the word of God of none effect through your tradition, which ye have delivered: and many such like things do ye" (Mark. 7:13).* Jesus calls the Old Testament the Word of God and in the same chapter He refers to the teachings of Moses as the commandment of God (Mark. 7:9-12). In the beginning of this chapter, we saw how Paul wrote that the Scriptures are inspired by God (2 Tim. 3:16-17). Jesus encourages his disciples to abide in His words, which are written within the gospels and then gets expanded on through the teachings of the New Testament letters. Peter indicates that the letters of Paul are inspired by God in the same way that the Old Testament is. When mentioning Paul and his letters, Peter writes:

"…our beloved brother Paul, according to the wisdom given to him, has written to you, as also in all his epistles, speaking in them of these things, in which are some things hard to understand, which untaught and unstable people twist to their own destruction, as they do also the rest of the Scriptures" (2 Pet. 3:15-16 NKJV).

Here, Peter puts the epistles of Paul on the same level as the Old Testament, and Jesus calls the Old Testament the Word of God. In other words, Jesus is the Word of God, but so is the Bible. As we have already seen, the Scriptures testify about Jesus and lead us into a deeper relationship with Him. When we are reading the Bible in communion with the Holy Spirit, the Author Himself is joining us to explain His Own Words to us.

Pictures of The Word of God Within the Scriptures

We have already seen how powerful the Word of God is in the life of the believer. God has given us some prophetic pictures of what the Word is, how it manifests and what it accomplishes in our lives. It always inspires and encourages me to ponder and pray over these pictures, since they reveal the power of the Word of God. We are going to end this chapter by looking at some of these pictures. It is exciting to study how deeply and powerfully the Word operates within us. The Word of God is described like:

a. **A Double-Edged Sword:** *"For the word of God is living and powerful, and sharper than any two-edged sword, piercing even to the division of soul and spirit, and of joints and marrow, and is a discerner of the thoughts and intents of the heart" (Hebr. 4:12- 13 NKJV).*

b. **A Fire and a Hammer:**
"Is not my word like as a fire? saith the LORD; and like a hammer that breaketh the rock in pieces" (Jer. 23:9)?

c. **Rain and Dew:** *Listen, you heavens, and I will speak; hear, you earth, the words of my mouth. Let my teaching fall like rain and my words descend like dew, like showers on new grass, like abundant rain on tender plants (Deut. 32:1-2 NASB).*

d. **A Lamp and Light:** *"Thy word is a lamp unto my feet, and a light unto my path" (Ps. 119:105).*

e. **Bread:** *"It is written, Man shall not live by bread alone, but by every word that proceedeth out of the mouth of God" (Matt. 4:4).*

f. **Milk:** *"But the word of the Lord endures forever." And this is the word which was preached to you. Therefore, rid yourselves of all malice and all deceit and hypocrisy and envy and all slander, and like newborn babies, long for the pure milk of the word, so that by it you may grow in respect to salvation, if you have tasted the kindness of the Lord" (1 Pet. 1:25-2:3 NASB).*

g. **Water:** *"…as Christ also loved the church, and gave himself for it; that he might sanctify and cleanse it with the washing of water by the word" Eph. 5:25-26).*

h. **Seed:** *"being born again, not of corruptible seed, but of incorruptible, by the word of God, which liveth and abideth forever" (1 Pet. 1:23).*

i. **A Mirror:** *"Anyone who listens to the word but does not do what it says is like someone who looks at his face in a mirror and, after looking at himself, goes away and immediately forgets what he looks like. But whoever looks intently into the perfect law that gives freedom, and continues in it—not forgetting what they have heard, but doing it—they will be blessed in what they do" (James 1:23-25 NIV).*

It is very encouraging to pray and meditate over the pictures of the Word of God in the Bible. His Word is effective and powerful to accomplish everything that the Father has sent it to do. It will not return without effect. We are transformed into the image of

Christ by abiding in His Word, under the guidance of the Holy
Spirit.

CHAPTER 6: THE WORD OF GOD AND OUR HEART

In the previous chapter we looked at how we can encounter Jesus through the Scriptures, and how the Word of God transforms us as we see more of Him. In this chapter we will continue our study on this topic, by looking at the power of receiving the Word of God in an open and well-prepared heart. The heart of the matter is always the matter of the heart. When Jesus taught on the Word of God and our hearts, He really brought the state of our heart to the forefront. For a deeper study of the overall importance of the heart, see my previous book *Abiding in the Father's Love*.

Lessons from the Parable of the Sower & the Soils

There is one parable of Jesus that we need to pay close attention to, when considering in what manner we are to receive the Word of God. That parable is the one about the seed and the different soils. This parable is included in all three synoptic gospels, which underscores its importance to us (Matt. 13:3-9, 18-23, Mark. 4:1-20, Luke 8:4-15). Jesus questions how it is possible to understand any of His other parables if we don't know this one (Mark. 4:13). This parable is a key that unlock the rest of His teachings.

Jesus shares this parable to illustrate how the Kingdom operates, and He reveals that it is like a man who goes out to sow seeds. These seeds fall on different grounds, and the type of ground it lands on determines if the seed will take root and grow or not. When explaining this parable, Jesus reveals to His disciples that the seed itself is the Word of God. He also lets us know that the different grounds represent different kinds of hearts. What state the heart is in will determine if the Word will grow or not. These are the four different kinds of hearts that Jesus addresses within this parable:

- **A heart that lacks understanding:** The first heart is the one that lacks understanding. The type of understanding that is lacking here is not information or knowledge, but the kind of revelation that come from an honest desire to know God. Jesus says: *"The sower sows the word. These are the ones who are beside the road where the word is sown; and when they hear, immediately Satan comes and takes away the word which has been sown in them"* (Mark. 4:14-15 NASB). As soon as the Word of God is being preached, the devil can steal it because without spiritual insight, the Word can't land and take root. For the word to bear fruit in our hearts, we need to have a desire to know Jesus more. If not, the devil will steal the Word and we will be blinded to its true meaning. This is what happened to pharisees and the religious leaders. They possessed knowledge of the Word, but they had no revelation because they didn't want to come and receive life from Jesus. Remember that the Bible was given to lead us into encounters with Jesus. It is only through Him that revelation can grow.

- **A shallow heart:** The shallow heart receives the Word of God joyfully at first, but because of the lack of depth in the believer's relationship with God, as soon as there is a price to pay or if resistance arises that challenges the truth of the Word, it is lost. Jesus describes this scenario as follows: *"And in a similar way these are the ones sown with seed on the rocky places, who, when they hear the word, immediately receive it with joy; and yet they have no firm root in themselves, but are only temporary; then, when affliction or persecution occurs because of the word, immediately they fall away"* (Mark. 4:16-17 NASB).

Spiritual growth has nothing to do with the excitement of the moment when someone receives the truths of the gospel, but it is all about how deep the roots of His Word can penetrate our hearts. If the Word of God has not been allowed take root in the depths of the believer's heart, as soon as there is a price to pay to hold on to it, the Word is lost and these people walk away. This doesn't have to mean losing one's salvation. In this context, it could also mean losing the spiritual reality and impartation of life that a revelation of the Word always brings.

- **A heart ensnared by the cares of this world:** This type of heart belongs to a believer who has lost his or her pure love for Jesus and instead has been seduced and snared by the things of this world. Jesus tells us: *"And others are the ones sown with seed among the thorns; these are the ones who have heard the word, but the worries of the world, and the deceitfulness of wealth, and the desires for other things enter and choke the word, and it becomes unfruitful"* (Mark 4:18-19 NASB). If our heart is filled with the lust for wealth and the worries about life, or even a desire for the good life that the world has to offer, there is little or no room for the Word of God to grow. The promises and revelation sown into this type of heart will be choked out and the Word will remain unfruitful.

- **A heart that is good soil:** This is the kind of heart that has been soaked in the love of the Father and is filled with a revelation of Jesus. I believe that this describes the heart of you who are reading this book. Jesus has given a wonderful promise for us whose heart is good soil for the Word of God: *"And those are the ones sown with seed on the good soil; and they hear the word and accept it and bear fruit, thirty, sixty, and a hundred times as much"* (Mark 4:20 NASB). If our heart is good, the Word will produce fruit within it. We don't have to strive for it to happen because the Word of God is living and active. It always produces that which it was sent to accomplish.

Our part is to abide in the love of the Father and always desire a deeper revelation of Jesus Christ. When we do that, the growth of the Word within our hearts will happen effortlessly. We will receive from the life of Jesus through the Word of God, so that healing, restoration, and transformation can happen while we're reading it. It can even create a reformation among the people of God through us.

The Process of Growth

Everyone who has put seed in the ground, knows that the seed doesn't instantly grow into a huge tree. It will take time for the Word of God to grow within our hearts. Jesus shares another parable that reveals this. I have referred to this parable in other parts of this book as well, only because it is so important to our understanding of spiritual growth: *"The kingdom of God is as if a man should scatter seed on the ground, and should sleep by night and rise by day, and the seed should sprout and grow, he himself does not know how" (Mark 4:26-27 NKJV)*. You need to make sure that the seed of the word is planted within the good soil of your heart.

You don't even need to know how it grows, or in which way it accomplishes what God wants. Like the farmer, the only thing we need to do is to trust the process, because the Word will bring forth a harvest within our lives: *"For the earth yields crops by itself: first the blade, then the head, after that the full grain in the head. But when the grain ripens, immediately he puts in the sickle, because the harvest has come" (Mark 4:28-29 NKJV)*. We need to remember this, so that we are not discouraged if it takes time for the Word of God to manifest in our lives. It will take time because God always works through processes, but we can be sure that it will happen because our Father always keeps His promises.

The Destructive Power of Religious Traditions

In the previous chapter we read a remarkable statement made by Jesus. When speaking to the pharisees about religious traditions, Jesus told them that they were *"…making the word of God of none effect through your tradition, which ye have delivered: and many such like things do ye" (Mark. 7:13)*. Religious traditions are the most effective way for Satan to keep our heart from being good soil. The thorns and the rocky place are a very revealing picture of the effects religious traditions have on our heart. Religion chokes the Word of God and hinders it from taking root within us.

We have seen how the Word of God is living and powerful to accomplish everything whereto the Father has sent it. But still the religious traditions can make the Word of God of no effect. One of my constant prayers has been that God would expose and deliver me from every belief and doctrine I hold to, that is based on religious tradition. I want to have revelation from the heart of the Father and to experience the full effect of the Word of God without anything that blinds me to it. The truth is that we all need to be set free from religious traditions from time to time so that we can grow in revelation and freedom.

King Josiah Rediscovered the Word of God

There is one man whose life reveals how powerfully the Word of God can operate within the person who receives it in a good and humble heart. That man is king Josiah. He was one of the last kings in Judah, but during his time as king, Judah experienced a national revival because of the king's love for the Word of God. I highly recommend that you read through his story all at once. You find it in 2 Kings chapters 22-23 and in 2 Chronicles chapters

34-35. Already as an eight-year-old, Josiah became king in Judah and at that time he started to seek the Lord. When he had reached the age of twelve, he destroyed the places assigned to worship of false gods all over the country. Josiah was a righteous king who had given himself wholeheartedly to God (2 Chron. 34:1-7).

When king Josiah had reigned for eighteen years, he began the work of repairing and restoring the temple in Jerusalem. During this process of restoration, a priest by the name of Hilkiah found the book of the Law (2 Chron. 34:8-18). It seems like the Word of God had been lost and forgotten by the people of God for some time, but now it was brought back to Josiah: *"Moreover, Shaphan the scribe informed the king, saying, "Hilkiah the priest gave me a book." And Shaphan read from it in the presence of the king. When the king heard the words of the Law, he tore his clothes" (2 Chron. 34:18-19).* Josiah humbled himself as he heard the Word of God and as a result the whole nation was brought into revival. We can learn a lot by looking at the way Josiah responded to hearing the Word of God:

- King Josiah asked for guidance and prayer through Huldah the prophetess (2 Kings 22:11-20, 2 Chron. 34:20-30).
- King Josiah and the people of Judah made a covenant with God to honor His Word (2 Kings 23:1-20, 2 Chron. 34:31-33).
- King Josiah celebrated the Passover (2 Kings 23:21-27, Chron. 35:1-19).

Not every king responded like Josiah when they heard the Word of God, which is why it could not operate as powerfully within the people of Judah during their reign. So, what was so special about king Josiah? We find the answer by reading a statement by the prophet Huldah concerning king Josiah's heart: *"Because your heart was tender and you humbled yourself before God when you heard*

His words against this place and its inhabitants, and because you humbled yourself before Me, tore your clothes, and wept before Me, I have indeed heard you," declares the Lord (2 Chron. 34:27 NASB see also 2 Kings 22:18-19). Because king Josiah had a humble and tender heart before God, the Word of God could shape his life in a powerful way. This is one of the best examples of the potential of a heart that is good soil in the Bible. All of Judah was brought into revival because the king humbled himself before God!

Learning from the Example of Josiah

Since king Josiah lived during the Old Covenant, his relationship to God and the conditions by which God related to His people were very different back then. We live in a much better covenant and our relationship with the Father is much better. We are His children and we have access to our Father all the time. Still there are some important lessons we can learn from the life of king Josiah. The most important is for us to rediscover and fall in love with the Word of God again. Another important lesson is that the Word of God only bears fruit in a humble and willing heart.

King Josiah received the Word of God so powerfully because his heart was good soil (2 Chron. 34:27). We need to have a heart like that as well. Jesus said: *"Blessed are the pure in heart, for they will see God" (Matt. 5:8 NASB).* A pure heart is humble and tender before God. We cannot shape our heart to become like that by ourselves, but the good news is that we don't have to. The Holy Spirit pours the love of the Father into our hearts and His love shapes our hearts so that we become pure, tender and humble before His Word. In that way, the Word can transform our lives and countless of other people's lives through us. God does not need believers who understand the Bible perfectly. He needs a humble heart that loves His Word. The Holy Spirit does the rest by breathing His life upon the written Word so that it becomes revelation to us.

My Experience of Encountering Jesus Through the Bible

My most powerful encounters with Jesus have always happened
through seeing Him in the Scriptures. I want to end this chapter
by sharing what the Word of God means to me. Reading the Bible
has always been a time of healing and comfort to me. It is when
I spend time in the Bible that I have my quality time with the
Father, Jesus and with the Holy Spirit. As I pray and meditate on
the promises of God, I dive deep into the love of the Father to see
more of His heart. The Words of Jesus have revived my heart so
that I have become filled with life and faith. When I got saved, I
had a very broken identity and my heart was so wounded that I
had shut it down just to survive. Reading the Bible to encounter
Jesus has been a major key to my identity being restored and my
heart being healed. I experienced how Jesus sent His word and
healed me and saved me from destruction (Ps.107:20 NASB). The
impartation of life and healing that the Word of God provides is
supernatural. The Scriptures are God-breathed and full of His
very substance and life. The time I spend in the Word has become
times of conversations with my best friend. Yet, it is so much
more because I meet Jesus within the Scriptures and get to listen
to His heart. He imparts His very own life and substance through
His Word. The Bible is such a wonderful gift to us and I love the
Word of God!

How to Read the Bible

There are several things that we could do that will help us when
studying the Bible. I am now going to share some of the things
that have been very helpful to me as I approach the Scriptures:

1. **Read the Bible Together with the Holy Spirit.**
    We have seen that the only way for us to understand the
    Bible is through a revelation from the Holy Spirit. When
    we are reading the Bible, we should always do it with a

heart of prayer. Invite the Holy Spirit to illuminate the Scriptures and expect your time of Bible study to become a place of fellowship and intimacy with Jesus.

2. **Read to Encounter the Heart of the Father.**
Remember that the goal of studying the Bible is to know the heart of the Father. Ask Him to reveal Himself in the Scriptures and always keep as your main goal to know His heart. This will help you remember that you're not reading just to gain knowledge about God, or to find inspiration for the next sermon you're going to preach. You're reading the Bible to grow in intimacy with Jesus.

3. **Find the Time and the Place.**
I have found it very helpful to know when and where to read my Bible. I like to get up and read the Bible early in the morning. Most of the time, I wake up early before the rest of the family. I make myself a cup of coffee and sit at my favorite spot in the sofa, reading and praying the Scriptures. Not everybody finds the time to read in the morning, but to be consistent with your Bible reading it is very helpful to find a time and place that works for you. It should preferably be a quiet place where you can sit with the Bible and the Holy Spirit in silence.

4. **Praying the Different Pictures of the Word of God.**
In the previous chapter, I made a small list of some of the pictures of the Word of God that I found in the Bible. I have often meditated and prayed over these pictures, asking the Holy Spirit to show me more of what they mean and how the Word of God operates in my heart. For example, what does it mean that the Word is like fire or a hammer? How does that apply to my Bible study and my approach to the Word of God? This has helped me to see the beauty of the Word of God.

5. **Use a Bible Reading Plan.**

    I recommend that you use a plan to read the Bible. I have been following a daily bible reading plan for years now. You can find Bible reading plans in many places online. It is very beneficial to have a structured approach to reading the Bible. Otherwise, I have noticed that we can easily fall into the habit of only reading our favorite parts of the Scriptures while never reading some parts of it at all. When you chose a Bible reading plan that covers the whole Bible within a year, that means that you will read about four chapters every day. This daily habit will take about twenty minutes of your day, but you will get a great overview of the Scriptures.

6. **Meditate on and Pray over the Scriptures.**

    Another helpful way of knowing God through the Bible is to pray and meditate over a certain scripture. As I said earlier, I follow a daily bible reading plan and as I read, there is usually one or two passages that the Holy Spirit highlights to me. During the day, I keep that verse in my heart to meditate on it and pray over it, so that the Holy Spirit can bring more revelation out of that verse. I might look at it again on my phone a couple of times, or just be quoting it in my mind and pray over it. This is how I get my daily bread through the Scriptures.

7. **Use Different Translations.**

    Another beneficial habit is to read different translations of the Bible. I'm usually reading three or four different translations of the New Testament every year, and two or more of the Old Testament. The reason for this is that the Greek and Hebrew language is so rich that there are several ways to translate different verses. I have found it very helpful to read different translations of the Bible, just to find some different nuances of the gospel. It's very helpful to read the same passage, but expressed in a little different way, so that it stays fresh. If you need help to find good translations to read, you find some of the ones that I like to use in the bibliography of this book.

8. **Find Good Bible Commentaries and Study Tools.**
    It is helpful to read commentaries on the different books of the Bible. You can find many good commentaries that has been written by theologians and biblical scholars. These commentaries provide historical background and cultural context to your Bible study. They give great help to understand the original meaning of the authors, and who they were writing to. For study tools, I recommend using a Strong's Concordance and Vine's Dictionary for studying the meaning of the Greek and Hebrew words. These are very helpful tools when you want to go a little deeper into the Bible and gain a better understanding of the meaning of certain Greek or Hebrew words.

There is more advice that could be added to this list. Feel free to explore different approaches to Bible study. The important thing is to remember that the Word of God always testifies about Jesus. When we read the Bible under the guidance of the Holy Spirit, He will lead us into a deeper relationship with the Father and a greater revelation of Jesus.

CHAPTER 7: BEING A WORSHIPPER IN SPIRIT & TRUTH

"But the hour cometh, and now is, when the true worshippers shall worship the Father in spirit and in truth: for the Father seeketh such to worship him. God is a Spirit: and they that worship him must worship him in spirit and in truth" (John 4:23-24).

One of the Father's greatest desires is to have sons and daughters who worship Him in spirit and truth. Becoming a worshipper is a fruit of encountering the love of God and beholding the beauty of His holiness. Worship in spirit and truth will always come as the spontaneous response of truly seeing Him as He is. This has nothing to do with a certain style of music, or a certain expression of praise. Being a worshipper is a posture of the heart. It means having a heart that is longing to give God all the glory. When we worship God, we are being transformed because it is then that we are beholding Him with unveiled faces. The atmosphere of a room that is filled with worship is the atmosphere where we find true freedom in the spirit. Paul wrote: *"Now the Lord is that Spirit: and where the Spirit of the Lord is, there is liberty. But we all, with open face beholding as in a glass the glory of the Lord, are changed into the same image from glory to glory, even as by the Spirit of the Lord"* (2 Cor. 3:17-18).

The Difference Between Praise & Worship

Worship has sometimes been confused with praise, but there is an important difference. Basically, they are two sides of the same coins since both flows from a worshipping heart. Because of this, we're only going to define the difference between them in a few short words here.

- *Praising God* is to sing and declare things about God, who He is and all the marvelous works that He has done. Songs of praise are songs that declare something about God. Praise is wonderful because we are reminded of the greatness of our loving Father and His marvelous works. Declarations of praise is also a very powerful weapon in our prayer and intercession as well. It shifts the spiritual atmospheres and releases the power of God.

- *To worship* is to sing songs of love and adoration to God. Worship is always directed directly to God, where we sing to Him. As we are beholding His amazing love and the beauty of His holiness, we will become worshipers.

Both praise and worship are very valuable, but as already stated, we don't need to make much to of the distinction between them, since both praise and worship is born from a heart that worships the Father in spirit and truth.

Worshipping the Father in Spirit & Truth

The Father desires for all His children to worship Him in spirit and truth. Jesus made this statement to the woman at the well, to show her the meaning of true worship. When Jesus was teaching on prayer, He gave us the Lord's prayer, and in it, He taught us to worship the Father: *"After this manner therefore pray ye: Our Father which art in heaven, Hallowed be thy name… For thine is the kingdom, and the power, and the glory, forever. Amen"* (Matt. 6:9, 13). The heart of everything that Jesus did in his ministry was to bring a clear revelation of the Father to the world, so that He would be known and glorified. In His high priestly prayer, Jesus revealed His motivation for ministry when He told the Father that *"… I have glorified thee on the earth: I have finished the work which thou gavest me to do"* (John 17:4).

The ministry of Christ was meant to reveal and glorify the Father. Jesus is longing to have a church that worship the Father in spirit and truth. When looking into the prayer life of Jesus, we find that He was continually worshipping and praising the Father. Here is one example:

"At that time Jesus said, "I praise You, Father, Lord of heaven and earth, that You have hidden these things from the wise and intelligent, and have revealed them to infants. Yes, Father, for this way was well pleasing in Your sight" (Matt. 11:25-26 NASB see also Luke 10:21, John 11:41-42).

An important part of living in Christlikeness is to worship and glorify the Father. When we encounter His love and see what an amazing Father He is, we cannot help but to praise and worship Him. In the same way, the Father wants everyone to worship the Son. This is the focus of the Holy Spirit as well. His ministry is always focused on revealing and glorifying Jesus and to lead us into joining the ongoing worship of the Lamb in the heavenlies (John 16:14). We get a glimpse of the heavenly worship in the fifth chapter of book of Revelation.

Worshipping the Lamb of God

The book of Revelation is a fascinating book. In this vision, the apostle John is taken into the heavens, where he enters the throne room of the Father. A scroll is brought forth, but no one is worthy to open it. John mourns over this, but one of the elders comforts John by telling him that the Lion of Judah is worthy to open it. As he turns to look at this mighty Lion, he sees the lamb of God, Jesus Christ (Rev. 5:1-7). Jesus is the only one who can open the scroll. When Jesus Christ finally does open the scroll the elders and the four living creatures respond by worshipping Him:

And when he had taken it, the four living creatures and the twenty-four elders fell down before the Lamb. Each one had a harp and they were holding golden bowls full of incense, which are the prayers of God's people. And they sang a new song, saying: "You are worthy to take the scroll and to open its seals, because you were slain, and with your blood you purchased for God persons from every tribe and language and people and nation. You have made them to be a kingdom and priests to serve our God, and they will reign on the earth" (Rev. 5:8-10 NIV).

The twenty-four elders and the four living creatures falls down in worship before king Jesus Christ, the Lamb of God. Then they worship Him by exalting His name and his finished work on the cross. They are singing a new song and as people who have been made a new creation in Christ, this is our song to sing as well. Jesus has purchased us with His blood and made us a kingdom of priests unto our God. As this is happens all the angels join to worship the Lamb of God:

Then I looked and heard the voice of many angels, numbering thousands upon thousands, and ten thousand times ten thousand. They encircled the throne and the living creatures and the elders. In a loud voice they were saying: "Worthy is the Lamb, who was slain, to receive power and wealth and wisdom and strength and honor and glory and praise (Rev. 5:11-12 NIV).

Finally, John saw that before the end of history, all of creation will worship the Lamb together with the angels, the four living creatures and the twenty-four elders of heaven:

Then I heard every creature in heaven and on earth and under the earth and on the sea, and all that is in them, saying: "To him who sits on the throne and to the Lamb be praise and honor and glory and power, for ever and ever!" The four living creatures said, "Amen," and the elders fell down and worshiped (Rev. 5:13-14 NIV).

This passage is so powerful that it almost feels unnecessary to comment on it. This is the key passage that sets the stage for the rest of the book of Revelation. The Father's plan is for all creation to worship the Lamb of God. We are participating in that plan every time we praise the name of Jesus. One day, every tongue will have to confess Jesus Christ as Lord, but we have the great privilege of being able to do it here and now! When we worship Jesus, we are touching the heart of the Father in a very deep way. Everything that He does is all about glorifying Jesus. The Son is just as focused on our praise to the Father. He is always calling us to worship the Father in spirit and truth. Love and generosity are always at the center of their relationship!

Worship & Deliverance

Worship has a powerful impact on our hearts as well. We can see this by looking at this famous passage from the book of Acts:

And at midnight Paul and Silas prayed, and sang praises unto God: and the prisoners heard them. And suddenly there was a great earthquake, so that the foundations of the prison were shaken: and immediately all the doors were opened, and every one's bands were loosed (Acts 16:25-26).

When the book of Acts describes how Paul and Silas sang praises in the prison it illustrates an important spiritual truth. One of the fastest ways to be delivered from bondages and oppression is to worship God. Living a lifestyle of worship will always equal living in freedom. God does not need us to worship Him. Jesus Christ is already exalted above all. Our worship does not change that, but it does radically change our perspective of reality.

It is amazing how our problems suddenly shrink and disappear when we worship God. The psalmist wrote that the worship of the Father's children, will break the power of the demonic attacks and give victory in spiritual warfare.

Let the high praises of God be in their mouth, and a two edged sword in their hand; To execute vengeance upon the heathen, And punishments upon the people; To bind their kings with chains, And their nobles with fetters of iron; To execute upon them the judgment written: This honour have all his saints (Psalms 149:6-9).

The devil has no weapon or counterattack that is effective against the pure worship of the people of God. I have seen this so many times while ministering to people who need to be delivered from spiritual oppression. If there is no breakthrough as we're praying for them, I usually start worshipping God. When an atmosphere of worship fills the room, we usually get breakthrough in prayer. The demonic realm cannot stand listening to how Jesus Christ is glorified. They must leave when we praise His name!

Silencing the Accuser

It is when we sing and declare the praises of God that our enemy is silenced. *"O Lord, our Lord, your majestic name fills the earth! Your glory is higher than the heavens. You have taught children and infants to tell of your strength, silencing your enemies and all who oppose you"* (Psalms 8:1-2 NLT). The devil is our accuser and he is constantly looking for ways to accuse us and to put us under a yoke of guilt and condemnation (Rev. 12:10). Because of the finished work of Jesus, his accusations are no longer valid (Col. 2:13-15). There is no condemnation for those who are in Christ. We can silence all the accusations of the devil by exalting the finished work of Jesus Christ. The reason for this is that the devil has no answer for the cross. He lost his voice when Jesus triumphed over Him there.

The desire of the Father is that His Son should be glorified. Every tongue will sooner or later confess Jesus as Lord (Fil. 2:9-11). But as we have already seen, we have the privilege of glorifying the name of Jesus here and now. His name is above every other name and a wonderful benefit of praising and worshipping the name of Jesus is that the accuser is silenced and loses his voice!

Worship Wins the Battle

In 2 Chronicles chapter 20, king Jehoshaphat was in a very critical situation. He was attacked by the armies of the Ammonites and Moabites. As a response, Jehoshaphat called the people to pray and fast, and God revealed the strategy to victory in the battle.

After consulting the people, Jehoshaphat appointed men to sing to the Lord and to praise him for the splendor of his holiness as they went out at the head of the army, saying: "Give thanks to the Lord, for his love endures forever (Chron. 20:21 NIV).

Jehoshaphat sent the worshippers ahead of the army to declare the everlasting love and grace of the Father. As a result, the battle was already over even before it had started. The people of God won an important victory that day. *"As they began to sing and praise, the Lord set ambushes against the men of Ammon and Moab and Mount Seir who were invading Judah, and they were defeated"* (2 Kings 20:22 NIV). The Lord had set up an ambush against the invading armies and they were defeated. This is a prophetic picture of the power of worship as a spiritual weapon. When we worship God, He will fight for us. The only thing that we need to focus on, is to collect the spoils of victory. Israel got so much spoil from this battle that is took three days to collect. In their case, the spoil was clothes, food and other valuable things (2 Chron. 20:25). In our case, the spoil to collect will be people getting saved, healed, and delivered. The reward of our victory is to extend the Kingdom of God. A worshipping lifestyle is an overcoming lifestyle!

The Discipline & Sacrifice of Worship

Worship is not something we do just because it feels good for us, but we do it because God is good. He deserves our worship and living a lifestyle of worship is a spiritual discipline. Many times, worship is connected to a spiritual sacrifice: *"Through Him then, let's continually offer up a sacrifice of praise to God, that is, the fruit of lips praising His name" (Hebr. 13:15 NASB).* By worshipping Jesus, we stay focused on who our Father is and we train our souls to abide in His love. We sometimes need to tell our soul to worship. In the psalms we find this principle illustrated many times. Here is one example of this: *"Why are you in despair, O my soul? Why have you become restless and disquieted within me? Hope in God and wait expectantly for Him, for I shall yet praise Him, The help of my countenance and my God" (Psalms 42:11 AMP).* When we are going through tough and stressful times, it is easy to forget that the best way to handle to handle the battle is to behold the glory of God in worship.

At times, we need to follow David's example and tell our soul to worship God. As we do that, we will find renewed strength and hope because the spirit of heaviness cannot survive when we put on the garment of praise. Isaiah prophesied that Jesus would bring in a new covenant, in which the children of God would receive *"…beauty for ashes, the oil of joy for mourning, the garment of praise for the spirit of heaviness; that they might be called trees of righteousness, the planting of the LORD, that he might be glorified"* (Isa. 61:3). We are living in that time now and when we worship the Lamb, we are being anointed with the oil of joy. As we receive a fresh anointing the spirit of heaviness is broken and we will be clothed in the garments of praise. The result will be that the Lord is exalted and glorified!

Worship & The Holy Spirit

Paul is encouraging us to *"… be filled with the Spirit; speaking to yourselves in psalms and hymns and spiritual songs, singing and making melody in your heart to the Lord; giving thanks always for all things unto God and the Father in the name of our Lord Jesus Christ"* (*Eph. 5:18-20*). There is a deep connection between living a Spirit-filled life and to have a heart of worship toward the Lord. As we have seen, the Holy Spirit always glorifies and lifts the name of Jesus high. When His presence fills our lives He will share that longing with us, which will result in us worshipping Jesus in words and deeds, but also by the way we speak to one another. This is one of the great blessings of being filled with the Spirit. Our hearts are transformed and filled with a renewed vision of Jesus and a deep desire to worship Him.

How to Cultivate a Heart of Worship

Worshipping in spirit and truth always starts with a revelation of God. As we encounter His love and the beauty of His holiness, we will respond by worshipping Him, but cultivating a lifestyle of worship is also a spiritual discipline. Here is some practical advice on how to cultivate a heart of worship:

1. **Living with a fresh revelation of who God is.**
    Worship in spirit and truth is always the response of a heart that has been captured by the love and goodness of God. When we see Jesus as He is, it impossible not to worship Him. Therefore, we should seek to live with a fresh revelation God. I usually do this by beholding Him in prayer and Bible passages that reveal His heart. I want my own heart to be expanded, so that I can see more of Him. A worshipper in spirit and truth is someone who has been captivated by the heart of the Father!

2.   **Keep a Trinitarian approach to worship.**
     The Father, the Son and the Holy Spirit all deserve our
     worship. I have always enjoyed worshipping all three
     persons of the Godhead. This keeps our worship fresh,
     since it is such a huge blessing to interact with all three
     different persons within the Godhead. In my experience,
     cultivating a deeper intimacy with each person within
     the Trinity creates a rich and deep relation with God.

3.   **Worship with the Book of Psalms and other Scriptures
     of worship.** One powerful way to learn how to live a
     lifestyle of praise and worship is by praying the psalms
     or other passages of Scripture that are written in the form
     of songs or prayers of praise and worship. By meditating
     on these passages and allowing the Holy Spirit to bring
     revelation out of them, we can learn how to express our
     worship in new and beautiful ways.

4.   **Find good praise and worship music.**
     We are blessed to live in a day when some of the most
     anointed psalmists and worship leaders in history are
     alive. Today, we can very easily download most of their
     material to our electronic devices. I take full advantage
     of this blessing by making sure that I download fresh
     worship music regularly. In the morning, I like to take a
     prayer walk and while I do that, I'm always listening to
     worship in my earphones, filling my mornings with
     wonderful praise and worship. I highly recommend you
     take time for focused worship and praise every day. That
     will refresh your spirit and renew your inner life. Make
     sure to find the worship songs that resonates with your
     heart during your present season with God. In that way,
     your time of worship Him stays passionate and relevant
     every day.

5. **Fill your day with worship**.

   Another great way to cultivate a lifestyle of worship is to fill your day with the sound of worship. I have learned a lot about this from my wife. No matter what she is doing, she always playing worship music in the background. She fills our house with worship. I have realized that this helps us staying focused on the Father's heart. When you are working in the garden, or while driving to work and throughout the day, you can cultivate a lifestyle of praise and worship together with Jesus. I am convinced that by just listening to anointed music, our hearts are impacted by the sound and atmosphere of heaven.

CHAPTER 8: SOAKING IN HIS PRESENCE

The highest calling in the life of the believer is to know God and be known by Him. *"God is faithful [He is reliable, trustworthy and ever true to His promise—He can be depended on], and through Him you were called into fellowship with His Son, Jesus Christ our Lord"* (1 Cor. 1:9 AMP). We are called into fellowship with Jesus Christ. Responding to that calling can be done in several ways, but the heart of the matter is to spend time with Him. I have noticed that many believers have learned to come to God to intercede or pray for things, but prayer is much more than that.

Prayer is all about spending time together with Him, getting to know His heart in deeper and more intimate ways. By doing that we're cultivating an awareness of His presence that we can bring with us throughout the rest of the day. This is how we can pray without ceasing (1 Tess. 5:17). We cannot intercede and pray for prayer requests all day long, but we can abide in His love and be aware of His indwelling presence all the time. It is an amazing honor and privilege for us to have an ongoing relationship with the Father. Soaking will help us to stay aware of the reality that He is always with us.

Ministering to the Lord

Cultivating an awareness of His presence by spending time just being with him ministers to our hearts. In His presence, we find healing, comfort and encouragement. But when we are spending time with Him, we are touching His heart in a deep way as well. I believe this is what happened at the church in Antioch, when *"… they ministered to the Lord, and fasted, the Holy Ghost said, Separate me Barnabas and Saul for the work whereunto I have called them"* (Acts 13:2). The word for ministering to the Lord implies that we minister by fulfilling our priestly duties. We are now a Kingdom of priests who have been purchased with the precious blood of Jesus (Rev. 5:9-10). To minister to the Lord is more than something we do. This is who we are. We are His priests and we are called to minister to His heart by abiding in His love, offering the sacrifices of praise and worship to Him. As we're soaking in His presence, setting time apart to just spend time with Him, we are delighting His heart.

Soaking in His Presence

I mentioned a little earlier in this chapter that we can soak in His presence. I want to elaborate on what that means for a moment. Soaking simply means to be still in His presence. It is a form of prayer where we are just spending time, resting in His love. The way many people practice soaking prayer, is to lay down on the couch or a bed, usually while there is soft, instrumental worship music playing in the background. This type of prayer is not about interceding or doing things *for* God in prayer, not even so much doing things *with* Him. We are simply *being* still, knowing that He is God by receiving *from* Him. Soaking is simply a practice in allowing our Father to love us, and a training for our soul to get used to abide in His love.

Our Father always loves us and His presence is always with us. But because we live busy, fast paced lives where countless things are fighting for our attention, we do not always stay aware of His presence. This is why we need to quiet our souls by focusing our attention on Him. That is what soaking is all about. The Psalms is speaking about this type of prayer when it says, *"Be still, and know that I am God" (Ps. 46:10).* John is writing about this as well. His expression for soaking is that we are abiding in the love of God (1 John 4:16). We sometimes need to be still and make a conscious decision to spend quality time with Jesus. This is what the Bible means when it encourages us to wait upon the Lord.

Waiting upon the Lord

We looked briefly at the biblical concept of waiting on the Lord in chapter one of this book and there we saw that waiting on the Lord does not mean being passive. It does not mean just sitting there, waiting for what the Lord will do for us. Waiting on the Lord means to seek His face, abiding in His presence and soaking in His love. This is how we wait on the Lord and that requires our focused attention. Psalm 131 is a short psalm, but it describes perfectly what it means to be waiting on the Lord.

Lord, my heart is meek before you. I don't consider myself better than others. I'm content to not pursue matters that are over my head — such as your complex mysteries and wonders — that I'm not yet ready to understand. I am humbled and quieted in your presence. Like a contented child who rests on its mother's lap, I'm your resting child and my soul is content in you. O people of God, your time has come to quietly trust, waiting upon the Lord now and forever (Psalm 131:1-3 TPT).

When we wait upon the Lord, we leave the complex mysteries and wonders of our faith to God. We surrender the stress of life and the challenges we face into His hands, by actively choosing to quiet our souls before Him. We're resting like sleeping child on its mother's lap, receiving from His love. We are waiting on the Lord by being renewed and refreshed, while soaking in His grace and manifest presence.

Glorifying God by Enjoying Him

How precious is Your lovingkindness, O God! The children of men take refuge in the shadow of Your wings. They drink their fill of the abundance of Your house; And You allow them to drink from the river of Your delights. For with You is the fountain of life [the fountain of life-giving water]; In Your light we see light (Ps 36:7-9 AMP).

The Father's heart is full of loving kindness toward us. He wants us to be filled with His abundance and for us to quench the thirst of our soul in the river of His delight. Enjoying His presence is the highest form of worship. By doing so, we are recognizing that He is our God and declaring that He is the source of our lives. When we are soaking in His presence, we are training our hearts to abide in a state of continually enjoying Him. As mentioned earlier, it is very common that people practice soaking prayer by laying down on the bed or on the couch, usually combined with listening to worship music suited for soaking prayer. But we can practice soaking prayer while taking a walk or when sitting on the bus as well. His presence never leaves us and we can stay aware of it all the time. The reason that we need set times for this is to train our hearts to stay aware of His presence. He is always present with us and by soaking we learn to be present with Him.

Mary is Our Example

Jesus had a certain place He loved to visit. That place was a house in Bethany, that belonged to some very good friends of Jesus. I am referring to the home of the Martha, her sister Mary and their brother Lazarus. One day while Jesus came to visit their home, something happened that illustrates what we are studying here. *"As Jesus and the disciples continued on their way to Jerusalem, they came to a certain village where a woman named Martha welcomed him into her home. Her sister, Mary, sat at the Lord's feet, listening to what he taught"* (Luke 10:38-39 NLT). Jesus was teaching His disciples, but Mary was also sitting at His feet listening together with them. By doing so, she took the posture of being the Lord's disciple. This was a very bold move because Rabbi's did not teach women in that culture. They were only teaching the men, so when Jesus allowed this to happen, it reveals a lot about His view of women. Jesus shows us that women can respond to the calling of being disciples of the Lord just like the men could. The calling of God is not dependent on gender, but on the Lord's calling. He anoints and equips both men and women to whatever assignments He has for them.

Breaking with Cultural Expectations to Spend Time with Jesus

However, in that culture, allowing a woman to be a disciple was unheard of, which explains Martha's frustration in this situation. *"But Martha was distracted by the big dinner she was preparing. She came to Jesus and said, "Lord, doesn't it seem unfair to you that my sister just sits here while I do all the work? Tell her to come and help me"* (Luke 10:40 NLT). Her sister Mary did not want to align with the cultural expectations of the day by helping her sister. Instead, she broke the norm by placing herself at the feet of Jesus to listen to Him as His disciple.

Jesus answered Martha by defending Mary's choice to sit at His feet: *"But the Lord said to her, "My dear Martha, you are worried and upset over all these details! There is only one thing worth being concerned about. Mary has discovered it, and it will not be taken away from her"* (Luke 10:41-42 NLT). Our culture is different from theirs in so many ways, but to sit at the feet of Jesus requires that we break with our culture as well. The stress and frantic pace of life in the western world makes it hard to wait upon the Lord. We need to make a conscious decision to break with the high pace of our day and instead choose the good part by waiting upon the Lord.

My Break with the Culture of Busyness in Ministry

When I had been working as a local pastor for a couple of years, I noticed that many of the leaders and ministers that I knew, were complaining about not being able to prioritize their relationship with God because of all the practical and social duties that came with pastoring a local church. Because I kept hearing about this, I made a quality decision to always have time planned into my schedule to spend time with the Father. Not just on my free time, but during my working hours as well. I still do it to this day. That was a bit challenging for some people, since they expected me to do a lot more active work. I had to break with these expectations because I know that we cannot do spiritual work can't in human strength.

Only by the anointing of the Holy Spirit can we do true Kingdom work, and the only place where we can receive a fresh anointing is in the secret place with our heavenly Father. This is the pattern that the apostles followed as well. When the practical needs grew in the early church, they realized that they could not afford to get stuck in practical work if they were to operate effectively in their calling. They gave this task to other trusted and anointed people, so that they could devote themselves to the Word and prayer: *"Instead, brothers and sisters, select from among you seven men of good reputation, full of the Spirit and of wisdom, whom we may put in charge of this task. But we will devote ourselves to prayer and to the ministry of the word" (Acts 6:3-4 NASB).* Their focus was to wait upon the Lord and the apostolic work that followed was a manifestation of their life with the Father.

The Benefit of Praying in Tongues

One of the ways through which we can quiet our minds and find rest for our souls is by praying in tongues. When we're praying in the spirit, our spirit is active while our minds and thoughts are put to rest. *"For if I pray in an unknown tongue, my spirit prayeth, but my understanding is unfruitful" (1 Cor. 14:14).* Praying in other tongues has been one of the most important ways through which I have deepened my intimacy with God. It is often as I take time to pray in the Spirit that I receive revelation and guidance from God. Praying in tongues has helped me to find peace and rest in my relationship with the Father, because it silences the voices in my mind and quiets my heart. By praying in tongues, we build ourselves up so that we can abide in the love of the Father. *"But ye, beloved, building up yourselves on your most holy faith, praying in the Holy Ghost, keep yourselves in the love of God, looking for the mercy of our Lord Jesus Christ unto eternal life" (Jude 1:20-21 see also 1 Cor. 14:4).* Finding rest for our mind, being edified, and built up, are certainly huge blessings of praying in tongues. But the greatest blessing of praying in tongues is that we stay connected to the love of the Father. Our spirits are speaking mysteries to God and that deepens our intimate relationship with Him. I love to spend time with Jesus by praying in the spirit.

People Will Notice That We Have Spent Time with Jesus

We have seen how soaking in the love of the Father touches and transforms our hearts and this is one of the ways through which we are ministering to Him. There is another important fruit of us spending time with Jesus, which is that other people will notice that something is different with us. Jesus will be seen, felt and experienced through us as we spend time in His presence. When Peter and John were brought in to be questioned by the religious council in Jerusalem, they observed something interesting with the two apostles:

"The council members were astonished as they witnessed the bold courage of Peter and John, especially when they discovered that they were just ordinary men who had never had religious training. Then they began to understand the effect Jesus had on them simply by spending time with him" (Acts 4:13 TPT).

These council members were not friendly toward the church and the gospel of Jesus Christ. In fact, they looked for reasons to charge the apostles with blasphemy and execute them. Yet, when they interrogated the apostles, they had to admit the powerful effect it had on them that they had spent time with Jesus.

When we spend time soaking in His presence people will take notice. They will be able to smell and taste Jesus Christ through our lives. I have experienced this many times as I have spent time with people who live their life in deep communion with God. The beauty of Christ shines forth through their lives. I have seen this in my own life as well. There have been several occasions when strangers have walked up to me in the street and asked me to pray for them because they have felt that "there is something special with me". As we abide in His presence people will be touched and ministered to by just being close to us. Jesus is very attractive and as we spend time with Him, people will be drawn to us so that we can share the love of God with them. This is what it means to be a witness for the Lord. We share with our lives what we have seen and experienced while soaking and abiding in the love of the Father (Acts 1:8).

How to Soak & Wait Upon the Lord

We are always surrounded by the presence of our loving Father and Jesus is always with us. There are several things we can do to cultivate a lifestyle of soaking and waiting on God.

1. **Make time for soaking prayer.**
    To develop a lifestyle of soaking in the presence of God, we need to be consistent, which means that we need to make time for soaking prayer several times a week, or even daily. A soaking session doesn't need to keep going for hours at a time, but thirty minutes, four times a week might be a good way to start. Lay down in a comfortable place and put your phone in flight mode. Put on a CD with still worship music and set the alarm to go off in thirty minutes. Then just lay still in His presence and enjoy His loving kindness. This is not the time for you to pray and intercede for things, but a time to be still before Him.

2. **Get rid of the mental distractions.**
    When we're soaking in the Father's presence, it is easy
    to get distracted. All kinds of thoughts will go through
    your mind as you try to soak. Ordinary things like what
    to cook for dinner, when to drive the kids to school, or
    the appointment with the doctor later in the week. Or it
    might even be prayer requests and other things that are
    important to you. You need to give these things to God
    to quiet your mind. You can do that by talking to Him
    about it, or by writing down your prayer requests which
    you can pick up to pray for later. It is important to quiet
    yourself and open your heart. so that you can focus on
    the heart of the Father.

3. **Find some good music suited for soaking.**
    There is a lot of very good music that has been recorded
    for soaking sessions. You can find most of this material
    online. You can also use regular worship music, but in
    case you want to do that, make sure that the songs on
    your playlist are peaceful and soft. I suggest that you use
    instrumental worship music. Many people have found
    that to be particularly helpful when it comes to soaking
    in the presence of God.

4. **Make waiting on God a regular ingredient of your
    prayer life.** When I started practicing waiting on God, I
    developed a habit that was very helpful and that might
    be useful for you as well. I took a walk for an hour every
    morning and the first half of that hour, I did not pray for
    anything. I told the Father that I wanted to take a walk
    with Him and listen to His voice. The last half of that
    hour I prayed in tongues under my breath while I kept
    my focused attention on Him. This was a helpful practice
    to learn the art of abiding in His presence and listen for
    His voice.

5. **Keep an awareness of His presence throughout the day.** The Father's presence is not leaving when your time of prayer is over. He promised to abide with you forever and He wants to keep talking to you throughout the day. As you stay consistent in practicing soaking prayer and waiting on God, you will develop the habit of practicing His presence throughout the rest of the day as well.

This is one of the shorter chapters in this book, but soaking and waiting on God has been one of the most important ingredients of my devotional life. It has helped me cultivate a lifestyle and a ministry that is centered around His presence, but the greatest blessing is that I can fellowship with Him every moment of every day!

CHAPTER 9: FASTING TO GAIN FOCUS AND CLARITY

Jesus expects fasting to be a normal part of every believer's life. This becomes clear by reading some of His statements on fasting and intimacy with God. This is a good example:

Moreover when ye fast, be not, as the hypocrites, of a sad countenance: for they disfigure their faces, that they may appear unto men to fast. Verily I say unto you, they have their reward. But thou, when thou fastest, anoint thine head, and wash thy face; that thou appear not unto men to fast, but unto thy Father which is in secret: and thy Father, which seeth in secret, shall reward thee openly (Matt. 6:16-18).

Jesus did not say, *"if you fast"*. Instead, He said, *"when you fast"*. This points to the fact that fasting is a natural part of our lifestyle as believers. A few chapters later He addresses fasting again. The reason was that some of John the Baptists disciples came to Jesus, wondering why it was that both they and the Pharisees fasted, but the disciples of Jesus did not. Here's how Jesus responded: *"How can the guests of the bridegroom mourn while he is with them? The time will come when the bridegroom will be taken from them; then they will fast"* (Matt. 9:15 NIV). Jesus told them that His disciples were not in a season of fasting during the time He was with them, but that there would come days when His disciples would be fasting. We are living in those days right now. As we will see in this chapter, fasting was a common practice in biblical times and it was practiced by many of the biblical characters that now have become our heroes of faith. Even today, fasting is a beautiful way for us to respond to the love of the Father. A lifestyle of fasting is a pathway to connect with the heart of Jesus, and it releases many blessings and benefits.

Defining Fasting

We can benefit from many different types of fasting. We can fast from social media, social interactions or watching television. But when the Bible speaks about fasting, it is referring specifically to abstaining from food for a period to focus on God. There are no specific instructions in the Bible about how long to fast, but we have some biblical examples of people fasting for certain number of days. I have listed some of these examples here:

- **The Forty day fast.**
  Moses fasted forty days when he was on mount Sinai to spend time with God. It was during this forty day fast he received the tablets of stone with the ten commandments (Exod. 34:28). Elijah fasted forty days as he fled into the desert to mount Horeb. (1 Kings 19:8). Jesus also fasted forty days as a preparation for His ministry. At the same time, Jesus fasted vicariously for our sake and blessed us with the result. Jesus overcame the temptations of Satan and broke the power of desert seasons, so that we could live in an eternal season of fruitfulness, enjoying rivers of living waters from the Holy Spirit (Matt. 4:1-11, Mark. 1:13, Luke 4:1-13).

- **The Daniel fast/ the Twenty-one day fast.**
  Daniel fasted for twenty-one days as a response to the prophetic declaration of Jeremiah that their 70 years of captivity were ending. It was time for the people of God to return to their promised land (Dan. 10:2-3). As Daniel prayed and fasted, he prayed through the plans of God for His people. Prayer and fasting can be very exciting!

- **The Fourteen day fast.**
  Paul fasted fourteen days while on the ship to Rome. This was not a fast that he chose, but during these two

weeks, Paul received a word from the Lord that gave hope and comfort to everyone on the ship(Acts 27:33-34).

- **The Ten day fast.**
  Daniel and his friends fasted for ten days, to not have to eat the Babylonian food, which would have made them unclean according to the law of Moses. Instead, they ate vegetables and drank water (Dan.1:5-17).

- **The Seven day fast.**
  The people of Jabesh fasted for seven days to mourn the death of king Saul (1 Sam 31:11). Fasting was a common expression of grief. David fasted for seven days when his child was sick (2 Sam. 12:16-23).

- **The Three day fast.**
  Queen Esther and the Jewish people fasted three days when facing the threat of being extinguished through the plot of Haman (Esth. 4:15-17). God saved them from the plot of Haman. Paul fasted three days after his encounter with Jesus on the road to Damascus (Acts 9:9).

- **Fasting for one day.**
  Not much is written on the topic of fasting in the law of Moses. In fact, there was only one specific day of fasting mentioned in the law. The people were commanded to fast for one day during the day of atonement (Lev. 23:26-32).

The reason that the Bible does not tell us exactly how long we are to fast, or what food to abstain from, is that we should be led by the Holy Spirit when in our personal fasting. The examples that I have listed above are given for our inspiration, but we should always be led by the Holy Spirit in our fasting. It is so easy to try to define our relationship with God through religious structures and fleshly efforts, since it gives us an illusion of control. But God wants a living and dynamic relationship with us.

Biblical Reasons for Fasting

The same could also be said about the reasons for our fasting. In the Bible we find several reasons to fast. We will now look at a biblical list of reasons to enter a fast, but this list is not meant to be turned into a routine or religious system. We should fast when we feel that the Spirit leads us to. Here are some reasons to fast that we find in the Word of God:

A. **Jesus Tells us to Fast** (Matthew 6:16-18, 9:15).
B. **To Humble oneself before God**
(1 Kings 21:27-29, 2 Chronicles 7:14, Ezra 8:21, Ps. 35:13 James 4:10).
C. **When Grieving**
(Judges 20:26, 2 Samuel 3:35, 1 Samuel 31:13)
D. **When Going through a Season of Repentance**
(1 Samuel 7:6, 2 Sam. 12:16-23, Nehemiah 9:1-2, Joel 2:12-13).
E. **For Spiritual strength and Winning Spiritual Battles**
(2 Chron. 20:1-4, Matthew 4:1-11).
F. **To Discipline the Flesh**
(1 Corinthians 9:27, 1 Corinthians 6:19-20).
G. **When Going into Deep Intercession**
(Ezra 8:23, Dan. 10:2-3).
H. **To Express our love and Worship to God** (Luke 2:36-37).
I. **To Wait on God and Receive Direction and Guidance from the Holy Spirit** (Acts 13:1-3, Acts 14:23, James 1:5).
J. **As a Preparation for Ministry and Appointing Leaders** (Acts 13:1-3, Acts 14:23, Matt. 4:1-11).

My Experience of Fasting

I have benefited immensely from my times of fasting. I have seen many powerful breakthroughs during my fasts, both in my own life and in our ministry. Suddenly, closed doors have opened and a greater measure of favor came upon our work. When we fast, we are denying our physical appetites for a time, to instead feed our spiritual man. This provides extra focus and clarity in our relationship with God. Fasting sharpens our spiritual focus and strengthens the vision God has given for our ministry. I have also seen the benefits of fasting in my personal life. During seasons of prayer and fasting, I have been delivered from habitual sins and spiritual bondages, but I have received a lot of inner healing and personal restoration as well. I usually receive a lot of revelation from Jesus during my fasts. We cannot earn anything from the Father by not eating, but He honors us when we seek for more of Him wholeheartedly. When we give Him our focused attention, good things will always happen!

Intermittent Fasting as an Alternative

For the last couple of years now, I have practiced a lifestyle of intermittent fasting, meaning that I only eat during certain hours of the day, usually in the afternoon. I have a window where I eat during four to six hours of the day, and the rest of the day I'm in a fasted state. I love the clarity of mind and freedom in life that intermittent fasting has given to me. It has done wonders for my health as well. For many years I struggled with overeating and I weighed much more than what was healthy for a person of my size. Intermittent fasting has helped me to get rid of all that, so that I can live a much healthier lifestyle. This is a very interesting alternative for anyone who wants to live a fasted lifestyle, which provides many spiritual, mental and physical benefits.

A Balanced Approach to Fasting

There has been a lot of religious mindsets connected to fasting. It is important to realize that fasting has nothing to do with earning the blessings of God. But it has everything to do with us making a conscious decision to focus on Him. We need to remember this, since fasting is only mentioned a few times in the Word of God. Yet, fasting has sometimes been said to be the answer for almost everything in the life of the believer. We shouldn't exaggerate the importance of fasting, but neither do we need to ignore its many benefits. I encourage you to go back and review chapter four one more time while you are reading this chapter. The truths that you find there are important to keep in mind, especially for those of you who have been living in a performance-based mentality in connection to fasting. The reason that we experience blessing and receive a greater anointing from the Father during, or after a fast is not because we earned anything by not eating, but it is because when we focus on Him, our heart opens and it becomes easier for us to receive.

One time, many years ago, a woman gave me a prophetic word about fasting. During that time, she was a mentor to my wife and me. I fasted a lot during these days but this woman came with a word from the Lord: "Martin, the Lord wants you to stop fasting. The devil has turned your fasting into a religious yoke and Jesus wants to set you free"! Then she prayed for me and broke this yoke. My periods of fasting had become a religious performance. After this happened, I didn't fast for a couple of years. Today I have a much more balanced approach to fasting and my fasts has once again become a source of blessing to me!

Wrong Motivations for Fasting

Whenever Jesus is teaching on spiritual disciplines, it is obvious that the most important thing to Him is our motivation. We are instructed not to fast to impress people by showing them that we are prayer warriors, who has "black belt in spiritual warfare and intercession". Jesus said: *"When you practice some appetite-denying discipline to better concentrate on God, don't make a production out of it. It might turn you into a small-time celebrity but it won't make you a saint" Matt. 6:16 The Message).* The fasting that we do to appear spiritual before God and to impress man that will not be helpful (Isa. 58:4-5). We should, if possible, keep our fasting between us and God. In that way we will not be tempted to try to impress people with our fast.

I love to do my fasting in this way. It feels very exciting to have a secret that is just between me and God. *"If you 'go into training' inwardly, act normal outwardly. Shampoo and comb your hair, brush your teeth, wash your face. God doesn't require attention-getting devices. He won't overlook what you are doing; he'll reward you well"* (*Matt. 6:17-18 The Message*). It is wonderful to have our secrets together with the Father, but we don't have to get religious about it. Early in my life with Jesus, I thought that just by mentioning that I was fasting, I would risk losing my reward. Because of this, I found myself in many awkward conversations where I became very creative in explaining why I didn't eat. My heart was right, so there was no need for me to worry about losing my reward. It would have been much better and a lot less awkward if I would have simply said that I was fasting.

Neither should we be fasting to gain extra favor with the Father. Being rewarded by the Father is not the same way as earning His approval. Rewards are given by grace because He loves to be generous with His gifts. Our only motivation for fasting should always be to respond to His love and desire to know Him better. We need good examples of people who show us what a life with God might look like. In the gospel of Luke, we find a very good example of living a lifestyle of fasting and prayer.

Anna Served God with Fasting & Prayer

Anna the prophetess had become an old woman, while Jesus still was a little child who was being brought into the temple. She was there when Joseph and Mary arrived with Jesus. *"Now there was one, Anna, a prophetess, the daughter of Phanuel, of the tribe of Asher. She was of a great age, and had lived with a husband seven years from her virginity; and this woman was a widow of about eighty-four years"* (Luke 2:36-37 NKJV). Anna is a forerunner when it comes to living a lifestyle of prayer and fasting. Even though very little is written about her, she is a prophetic role model that God has provided for everyone who is called to a life of prophetic intercession and fasting. She lived in the temple and served God in this way. Anna *"… who did not depart from the temple, but served God with fastings and prayers night and day"* (Luke 2:36-37 NKJV). Because of Anna's pure devotion to God, she was granted the honor to see Jesus as a little child, while He was being brought into the temple. Anna carried a revelation about Jesus that had been born out of her life of intimacy with God. *"And coming in that instant she gave thanks to the Lord, and spoke of Him to all those who looked for redemption in Jerusalem"* (Luke 2:38 NKJV).

God is raising up people into similar ministries today; to serve the Lord and His people through a lifestyle of fasting and prayer. As we live in intimacy with the Father by cultivating a lifestyle of prayer and fasting, we will carry a deep revelation of Jesus and the plans and purposes of God. Even though we could find many reasons to fast, carrying a deep revelation of Jesus and to know the love of the Father in deeper ways is always the main thing.

Fasting & Ministering to God

In an earlier chapter, we looked at how we can minister to God by soaking in His presence. There we studied how the prophets and teachers in Antioch ministered to the Lord. They did that by spending time fasting together: *"As they ministered to the Lord, and fasted, the Holy Ghost said, Separate me Barnabas and Saul for the work whereunto I have called them. And when they had fasted and prayed, and laid their hands on them, they sent them away"* (Acts 13:2-3). The prophets and teachers of the church in Antioch were ministering to God and fasted together. As they spent time in His presence, the Holy Spirit led them to separate Barnabas and Paul into their calling as apostles. I believe that we find an important principle here. As the prophets and teachers learn how to minister to God in unity, we will see a powerful release of the apostolic ministry. It is powerful to combine waiting on God with fasting. Choosing to spend a day in the presence of the Father while we are fasting is always time well spent. This has been very fruitful for me, and it has helped me to grow in my relationship with God.

Fasting & Hearing the Voice of God

It is common for people to receive new revelation and instruction from the Holy Spirit while they're fasting. That was exactly what the leaders of the church in Antioch experienced. The Spirit told them to separate Barnabas and Paul for the work that the Father had prepared for them (Acts 13:2). The Holy Spirit doesn't need be convinced to speak to us, but sometimes we need to pull away from the distractions of life to hear what He is saying. Fasting is a good way to do this. When we don't have to focus on preparing meals and eating food, we get a lot of extra time and energy to focus on God. That makes it easier for us to listen to His voice.

Fasting & Separation to Ministry

Another important lesson to learn from Acts 13 has to do with fasting as preparation for new assignments or ministry. After the leaders in Antioch had received the leading from the Holy Spirit to separate Barnabas and Paul, they fasted, prayed and sent them out. Paul and Barnabas practiced this in a similar way when they ordained elders in the churches that they had planted. *"And when they had ordained them elders in every church, and had prayed with fasting, they commended them to the Lord, on whom they believed"* (Acts 14:23). It seems to have been a common practice in the early church to pray and fast as a preparation for ministry. Jesus was led by the Holy Spirit into the desert, where He fasted for forty days as a preparation to enter His ministry. *"Then Jesus was led up by the Spirit into the wilderness to be tempted by the devil. And when He had fasted forty days and forty nights, afterward He was hungry"* (Matt. 4:1-2 see also Luke 4:1-2). This is a biblical principle that we all could benefit from practicing when we are about to enter a new assignment from God.

I have personally chosen to fast as a preparation whenever I have been called to new things in the Kingdom of God. During these fasts, I have always received revelation and a fresh anointing for the work and challenges ahead of me. God responds as we set aside time to focus on Him, to receive guidance concerning the assignments that He has given us. The Father will release a fresh anointing upon us when we do that. Jesus is a powerful example of this. After His time of fasting *"… Jesus returned in the power of the Spirit into Galilee: and there went out a fame of him through all the region round about. And he taught in their synagogues, being glorified of all"* (Luke 4:14-15). Here we can find a biblical pattern. Jesus is our great example, so when we prepare for ministry by spending time in prayer and fasting, we will walk in the power of the Holy Spirit like Jesus did.

Fasting & Family

When Paul was writing to the different churches, he was giving a lot of practical advice concerning ordinary life. One such area that involved prayer and fasting in the family. Paul gave a very good advice to the married people in the church at Corinth: *"Do not deprive one another except with consent for a time, that you may give yourselves to fasting and prayer; and come together again so that Satan does not tempt you because of your lack of self-control" (1 Cor. 7:5 NKJV).* The reason that Paul gave this advice is that family life can at times be stressful and busy. Sometimes it might be a good idea to set a few days apart to pray and fast to clear our head and focus on God. Our relationship with the Father is never an excuse for not taking care of each other's needs, but there are times when husband and wife would do well to separate time for prayer and fasting. That is a blessing to the whole family. My wife and I do this every now and then and it has always been very fruitful. God honors us as we take time to focus on Him. Both our marriage as well as our children is rewarded when we spend time with Jesus in fasting and prayer.

Fasting & Deliverance

There is one more scripture that we need to address. The passage I am referring to is found in the gospel of Matthew. The disciples had failed to cast a devil out of a little boy. They asked him why they failed, to which Jesus responded: *"Because of your unbelief; for assuredly, I say to you, if you have faith as a mustard seed, you will say to this mountain, 'Move from here to there,' and it will move; and nothing will be impossible for you"* (Matt.17:20 NKJV). Then follows a particular verse that some translations have written into the text, while some only include it as a footnote: *"However, this kind does not go out except by prayer and fasting"* (Matt. 17:21 NKJV). The reason that some translations don't include it in the actual text is because it is not included in many of the oldest manuscripts. This is the case also in the gospel of Mark, where we can read about this same event (Mark 9:29) Even if Jesus said this, it is important to remember that He made this statement before the cross. This is significant because Jesus has defeated the devil and stripped him of all authority (Col. 2:15). We live on the other side of the cross and Jesus has delegated authority to us in His name (For a deeper study of this topic, see my book *Transformed by the Grace of God)*. Because of this, we are not required to pray and fast to have authority to cast out demons. But there are some powerful promises of blessings connected to keeping the Lord's chosen. We find many of these promises in the Book of Isaiah. In the next chapter, we will take a deeper look at these promises.

CHAPTER 10: THE BLESSINGS OF FASTING IN ISAIAH 58

In the book of Isaiah chapter 58, we find some powerful blessings connected to a lifestyle of fasting and prayer. Within this chapter, we will study them a little deeper, but first we need to look at the reason why this was brought up in the first place. It all starts with the people of God complaining that God did not seem to take notice of their fasting:

Why have we fasted and You do not see? Why have we humbled ourselves and You do not notice?' Behold, on the day of your fast you find your desire, and oppress all your workers. "Behold, you fast for contention and strife, and to strike with a wicked fist. You do not fast like you have done today to make your voice heard on high (Isa. 58:3-4 NASB)!

Fasting is not a magic formula. Just because we stop eating and start to pray more, it doesn't guarantee that Jesus gives us what ever we want. Fasting is meant to be a relational practice through which we focus our attention on the Father. By doing so we align with His will and partner with Jesus in what He is doing. In the last chapter, we saw that it is a bad idea to fast to gain extra favor from God. We have the Father's favor and we are His very own blessed and beloved children.

Fasting is a good way for us to partner with the Father, so that these blessings can manifest in our lives. This is how we make our voice heard on high. Since we are already seated with Christ in the heavenlies, this simply means that we're speaking with the Father. God was not impressed with the fasting practiced by the people of Judah because they had turned it into a religious ritual and a legalistic show: *"Is it a fast like this that I choose, a day for a person to humble himself? Is it for bowing one's head like a reed and for spreading out sackcloth and ashes as a bed? Will you call this a fast, even an acceptable day to the Lord"* (Isa. 58:5 NASB)?

The Fast that God Desires

After revealing that God is not impressed by their fasting, Isaiah goes on to declare the fast that God has chosen:

"Is this not the fast that I choose: To release the bonds of wickedness, to undo the ropes of the yoke, and to let the oppressed go free, and break every yoke? Is it not to break your bread with the hungry and bring the homeless poor into the house; When you see the naked, to cover him; And not to hide yourself from your own flesh" (Isa. 58:6-7 NASB)?

The fast that God has chosen consists of two important things.

- ***It brings freedom to the oppressed.***
- ***It transforms our hearts so that we learn to embrace a lifestyle of compassion.***

The bonds and yokes that Isaiah mentions in this passage are a picture of spiritual bondages and demonic oppression. When we fast, we should always expect a greater measure of our freedom in Christ to manifest. Oppression will be broken from all areas of our lives through the power of Jesus Christ. Breaking bread with the hungry and bringing the homeless into the house has a very literal application, but there is something deeper hidden within the text as well. This is a picture of helping the orphan to come home to the Father. To cover the naked is a picture of being filled with the love of the Father, which covers a multitude of sins and restores the fallen (1 Pet. 4:8). Our goal should always be to see people healed and restored from all damage, caused both by sin and personal failures.

The Benefits of Fasting

I want to list some of the blessings that is promised in Isaiah 58 to those who practice God's chosen fast. You will notice that all these blessings are part of our inheritance as God's children, so we do not earn them by our fasting and prayer. They manifest as we partner with the Father by giving Him our focused attention and by allowing Him to shape our lives. Here are the benefits of fasting that we find in Isaiah 58:

- **Revelation & Insight** *"Then shall thy light break forth as the morning"* (Isa. 58:8).
- **Healing & Restoration** *"And your healing (restoration, new life) will quickly spring forth"* (Isa. 58:8 AMP).
- **Protection & Security** *"Your righteousness will go before you [leading you to peace and prosperity], the glory of the Lord will be your rear guard"* (Isa. 58:8 AMP).
- **Answer to Our Prayers** *"Then shalt thou call, and the LORD shall answer; thou shalt cry, and he shall say, Here I am* (Isa. 58:9).
- **Deliverance From Darkness & Gloom into Light & Clarity** *"If you remove the yoke from your midst, The pointing of the finger and speaking wickedness, And if you offer yourself to the hungry And satisfy the need of the afflicted, Then your light will rise in darkness, And your gloom will become like midday"* (Isa. 58:9-10 NASB). You probably noticed that this promise comes with a condition. We will take a closer look at this in the next chapter.
- **Renewed Strength & Spiritual Life** *"And the Lord will continually guide you, and satisfy your soul in scorched and dry places, and give strength to your bones; and you will be like a watered garden, And like a spring of water whose waters do not fail.* (Isa. 58:11 AMP).

- **An Anointing & Grace for Restoration** *"Those from among you will rebuild the ancient ruins; You will raise up the age-old foundations; And you will be called the repairer of the breach, The restorer of the streets in which to dwell (Isa. 58:12 NASB).*

During my fasts, I read and pray through this chapter to remind myself of these blessings. By faith, I declare and believe for them to manifest to a greater degree in my life. These blessings have manifested in a greater way the last couple of years, but I'm still believing for an even greater manifestation of these blessings. There is a lot of freedom and joy in partnering with Jesus through prayer and fasting, especially when we consider all the blessings and benefits that we receive by doing so.

Fasting & Freedom from Yokes and Bondages

In the last chapter, we saw that we're not gaining more authority over the forces of darkness through prayer and fasting. Jesus has already won a complete victory over the devil, and He has given us delegated authority to cast out demons (Luke 10:18-20). There is still something to be said about fasting, spiritual warfare and finding freedom from spiritual oppression. When we're fasting, we become more sensitive and focused on Jesus. This makes it easier to discern how to pray for people in need of deliverance.

It is not a question of gaining more spiritual authority, but about being sensitive to the leading of the Holy Spirit in how to use our authority in Christ. This is the reason why so many people have found new dimensions of freedom while fasting. In fact, the fast that pleases the Father is one where deliverance from oppression takes place. Earlier in this chapter we discovered that the fast which the Father desires is one where the oppressed go free: *"[Rather] is this not the fast which I choose, To undo the bonds of*

*wickedness, To tear to pieces the ropes of the yoke, To let the oppressed
go free And break apart every [enslaving] yoke" (Isa. 58:6 AMP)*?

During times of fasting, the Holy Spirit wants to highlight areas
of oppression in our lives and lead us into even more personal
freedom. I had a profound experience of this many years ago. At
that time, it was obvious that I had strongholds of both fear and
a poverty-mentality in my life. This limited me from being as
fruitful as God wanted me to be, both in my ministry and in my
personal life. I was under a heavy yoke of oppression. During a
fast I was led by the Holy Spirit to break the yokes and bondages
in these areas. The effect of doing that manifested immediately.
I became much bolder and was delivered from the fear that had
previously tormented me. I found new dimensions of financial
blessing and provision as well. This had a big impact on my life
and I started to live out of my freedom in Christ in a much greater
way.

Fasting & Healing

There are obvious physical and mental benefits of fasting, but
among the effects of being delivered and set free from oppression
is that we are healed and restored on the inside as well. We read
from Isaiah 58 again: *"Then your light will break out like the dawn,
and your healing (restoration, new life) will quickly spring forth; Your
righteousness will go before you [leading you to peace and prosperity],
The glory of the Lord will be your rear guard" (Isa. 58:8 AMP)*. Many
times, while fasting, I have experienced healing encounters with
the love of the Father, where my heart was restored and new life
flooded my innermost being. When we spend focused time with
the Father this is inevitable, because just to be in His presence
and encountering His love is a deeply healing experience. I have
received many testimonies from people I have met in different
churches about healing in connection to fasting and prayer.

Who Should Not Fast?

As we have already seen, Jesus expects fasting to be an important part of every believer's life. That means that fasting is for almost everybody. There are some people who should be careful with fasting however, or in some cases maybe not practice fasting at all. There are people who have medical conditions, which make it impossible for them to fast. People who struggle with eating disorders should not fast either. If someone is planning to do a longer fast, it might be a good idea to ask a doctor for advice to decide what type of fast is best for that specific individual.

Being unable to fast does not equal missing out on the blessings of God. We need to remember that fasting is not a method to earn God's blessings. We have already inherited the fullness of our inheritance in Christ. If fasting from food could be damaging to your health, you can ask the Holy Spirit for other ways through which you can partner with Him. The point is relationship and intimacy with Him. Ask the Holy Spirit for help, and He will lead you into a dynamic relationship with Him.

How to Fast

Jesus encouraged His disciples to fast, but He did not give a lot of instructions on how to do it. Yet, there are some practical keys that have helped me, and I want to share some of them with you:

1. **Start with smaller fasts.**
   As always when starting a new habit, it is best to start by taking smaller steps. Starting the journey of fasting by skipping one or two meals a day is a good idea. When I started practicing fasting, I fasted that way. As I got used to shorter fasts, I increased the length of the fasts. Longer fasts are not better. We should follow the leading of the

Holy Spirit in how we plan our fasts. Start small and see where your journey of fasting will take you.

2. **Pick a day that is convenient.**
   It is easier to fast if you do it during a day when you can avoid distractions. Make sure to pick a day where you don't have to be at a lunch meeting, or anything else that involves gathering around a meal. In that way you avoid unnecessary temptations and awkward conversations. It is a good idea to use the time that is usually reserved for cooking and eating for prayer.

3. **Ask the Holy Spirit for instructions.**
   I have discovered that the Holy Spirit often gives me a scripture or a certain theme for my fasts. I like to enter my fasts well prepared, so I usually ask the Holy Spirit the day before I enter my fast, if He wants to give any instructions for that fast. I can then save time that can be better used in prayer. The day before you start your fast is a good time to ask Him for guidance and instruction.

4. **Meditate and pray over Isaiah 58.**
   I often take some time to read Isaiah 58 and the benefits and of fasting that are listed there. That helps me to stay connected to the heart of the Father while fasting, and it stirs my faith to see the blessings of fasting manifest even more in my life. I suggest that you read through Isaiah 58 at least once a day while fasting.

5. **Start and break a fast in a good way.**
   Before you start a longer fast, it is a good idea to speak to a doctor about how the body might be affected. Before you're entering a longer fast, try to eat a little less for a couple of days. Switch to food that is easier to digest, so that your body gets a chance to get used to be in a fasted

state. As you are breaking the fast, you do the same thing but in reverse. Start by eating small portions of food that are easily digested, and slowly get back to your normal eating habits. For periods of fasting up to three days, you can usually just stop eating when you enter the fast, and then start eating normally when the fast is over.

6. **Intermittent fasting.**
   As I mentioned earlier, I practice intermittent fasting as a lifestyle, which means that I am only eating during a window of time every day. To eat for eight, six or maybe five hours a day, and staying in a fasted state throughout the rest of the day, provides many huge benefits. These benefits will affect you both spiritual and mental, as well as physical. I wholeheartedly recommend all my readers to adopt a lifestyle of intermittent fasting. It is easy to find good information about intermittent fasting online. You can find many podcasts, books and other resources that will provide a good understanding on how to live a lifestyle of intermittent fasting as well.

7. **Stay committed to the time you have set for your fasting.** Your commitment to fulfill a fast will be tested. If you are not used to fast, your body will start to scream for food. Hunger usually comes in waves during times of fasting, so it is important to stand firm in the decision to fulfill the time that you have set for a fast. A good help in doing that is to drink a lot of water and to do some lighter physical activity during the fast. I always have a bottle of water available when I am fasting, and I usually take walks a couple of times during the day. That makes the hunger go away for me.

CHAPTER 11: THE JOY OF INTERCESSION

One of the most powerful ways to partner with the love of Christ is to pray and intercede for people, the church, the nations and whatever the Holy Spirit leads us to pray for. In that way, we are releasing the Kingdom of God in prayer, so that more people can encounter the Father's love. As always, Jesus is our example: *"Who is he that condemneth? It is Christ that died, yea rather, that is risen again, who is even at the right hand of God, who also maketh intercession for us"* (Rom. 8:34). Jesus has risen and is currently seated at the right hand of the Father. As our High Priest, Jesus is right now praying for us. In fact, interceding for His brothers and sisters has now become one of His main focuses. *"Wherefore he is able also to save them to the uttermost that come unto God by him, seeing he ever liveth to make intercession for them"* (Hebr. 7:25). Since we are in the process of being conformed into the image of Jesus, our hearts are gradually becoming more like His. His passions and interests are now becoming ours, which means that the more we grow into His image, our desire to intercede for our brothers and sisters will grow. This transformation of our hearts will take place in proportion to the progress of His work within us.

The Freedom in Being for People

To be an intercessor means that we are praying for people, which in turn means that we are standing with them for the will of God to break through. There is so much joy and freedom in standing with people. A big burden falls of our back when we realize that we don't have to have a bad attitude against the body of Christ, being irritated and critical toward churches and its leaders. It is much more fun to stand with them in prayer and intercession. We are on the same team and their victories are our victories, just like their challenges are ours as well. Through our intercession and prayer, we can release the will of God on their behalf.

When I hear about believers who are experiencing revival and blessings, I ask God to bless them even more. When I hear about believers that are facing difficult challenges, I pray that God will strengthen them. If I hear about the failure, sin, or brokenness of the body of Christ, I pray for healing and restoration to happen. Praying for our brothers and sisters is a wonderful privilege and a powerful way to release the love of God. It has been a great joy to grow in prayer for the people of God, but at the same time it is a burden that the Lord has put in my spirit. I wholeheartedly agree with the prophet Samuel and the statement he made while he was speaking to the people of Israel: *"Moreover as for me, God forbid that I should sin against the LORD in ceasing to pray for you"* *(1 Sam. 12:23).* I would consider it a sin to not carry the people of God in prayer, because I know how dear all of us are to the Father and how much it pleases Him when I pray for the body of Christ.

Heaven Is Serious About Our Prayer & Intercession

We saw in an earlier chapter how all of heaven worship the Lamb and how the heavenly beings continually glorify the Father. But there was one occasion when all of heaven went silent: *"When the Lamb broke the seventh seal, there was silence in heaven for about half an hour. And I saw the seven angels who stand before God, and seven trumpets were given to them" (Rev. 8:1-2 NASB).* For the heavenly worship and praise to grow silent like that, something important had to be happening. It is astonishing to find something that touched the heart of the Father so deeply that everything became quiet in heaven for half an hour. What could that be? We'll find the answer below:

Another angel came and stood at the altar, holding a golden censer; and much incense was given to him, so that he might add it to the prayers of all the saints on the golden altar which was before the throne. And the smoke of the incense ascended from the angel's hand with the prayers of the saints before God (Rev. 8:3-4 NASB).

As Jesus broke the seventh seal, our prayers and intercessions ascended before God, and all of heaven watched silently as this happened. Our prayers and intercessions are so precious to the Father. They touch His heart in ways that are too deep to even express with words. All the heavenly beings know this, so out of respect for the sacredness of the moment they went silent. As the answers to our prayers are hurled down to the earth, the whole world is shaken by the power of Jesus Christ. *"Then the angel took the censer and filled it with the fire of the altar, and hurled it to the earth; and there were peals of thunder and sounds, and flashes of lightning and an earthquake" (Rev. 8:5 NASB).* Through our prayer and intercession, we have the power to influence all of creation. Answering our prayers is of the highest importance to the Father. We are His children and we are His covenant partners through Jesus Christ. This might sound a bit dramatic, but as we will see, prayer is not complicated and we have a Helper that is more than qualified to lead us as we give ourselves to intercession.

Not Knowing How to Pray

Sometimes people tell me that they are not good at praying, so they have decided to leave the intercession to the "professional prayer warriors". The truth is that none of us knows how to pray. Paul writes: *"Likewise the Spirit also helpeth our infirmities: for we know not what we should pray for as we ought: but the Spirit itself maketh intercession for us with groanings which cannot be uttered"* Rom. 8:26). Just like Jesus, the Holy Spirit intercedes for us and He helps us to pray by guiding us and interceding through us. We will not become good at intercession by just knowing how to pray. We become intercessors by knowing the heart of the Father. Therefore, a good place to start when we want to pray for people is by realizing that we are not good at praying at all. That will give space for the Holy Spirit to guide us as we step into the flow of prayer. He is our Helper and part of His ministry is to help us in our prayer life.

Praying from Our Authority in Christ

Since we are now living in the New Covenant and Jesus has won a complete and eternal victory on the cross, we're not praying to get victory in the spiritual battle. We are praying from a position of victory and authority. The devil is already defeated and all the principalities and powers have been stripped of all their power and authority through the cross (Col. 2:15, Luke 10:18-20). Jesus has been given all authority and He has delegated that authority to us (Matt. 28:18-20). For this reason, we never need to question who is going to win. Jesus has already won the spiritual battle. Jesus is our High Priest, who is always praying for us. We are his royal priesthood, who have been called to proclaim His complete victory in the spiritual realm and to all of creation. *"But you are a chosen people, a royal priesthood, a holy nation, a people for God's own possession, so that you may proclaim the excellencies of Him who has called you out of darkness into His marvelous light"* (1 Pet. 2:9).

We are His royal priesthood and our ministry as his priests is to carry the burdens of the people to the Father in prayer. Our duty as his kings is to use our delegated authority to take the occupied ground back from the enemy. Because we stand with Jesus in His authority, we are now ruling and reigning with Him. We are to enforce his victory in the spiritual realm by destroying the works of the devil (1 John 3:8). Jesus is not only our High Priest, but He is our glorious King as well and we are His royal priests. This is the reason that Jesus is called: *"KING OF KINGS, AND Lord OF LORDS" (Rev. 19:17 NASB).* As children of God, we are his kings and lords, but Jesus is our King and Lord.

Carrying Each Other's Burdens

Live creatively, friends. If someone falls into sin, forgivingly restore him, saving your critical comments for yourself. You might be needing forgiveness before the day's out. Stoop down and reach out to those who are oppressed. Share their burdens, and so complete Christ's law. If you think you are too good for that, you are badly deceived (Gal. 6:1-3 The Message).

The true heart of all intercession is to bow down by reaching out to the oppressed in prayer. Through our prayers, we carry their burdens to the Father by asking Him to intervene on their behalf. I am blessed to have a team of intercessors who stands with me and share the burden of ministry by praying for me. When I see their hearts, I see Christlike hearts. A person who has learned to pray and intercede in the Holy Spirit will be the type of person who forgives and restores the one who has fallen into sin.

We should take John's advice to heart when he encourages us to pray as we see someone trapped in sin: *"If any man see his brother sin a sin which is not unto death, he shall ask, and he shall give him life for them that sin not unto death"* (1 John 5:16). If we stay focused on praying for other people, we will not have time to think of their sins and failures. Therefore, we will keep our critical comments and attitudes to ourselves. Since intercession comes from a place of brokenness and awareness of our own need of mercy and grace, the critical spirit will not be able to take root in our hearts when our focus is to carry one another's burden in prayer.

Turning our Criticism into Prayer & Receiving Healing

As we saw in the previous chapter, Isaiah 58 speaks about God's chosen. One of the things that we are encouraged to repent from is: *"The pointing of the finger and speaking wickedness"* (Isa. 58:9).

The pointing of the finger is a picture of critical and judgmental attitudes, or even a stronghold of the critical spirit. When we're removing that from our lives, healing will come quickly and we will become fruitful and strong in the Lord (Isa. 58:6-12). If we need healing and restoration, one of the ways through which this happens is by praying for other people. Job is an example of this. He was restored as he prayed for his friends. *"The Lord restored the fortunes of Job when he prayed for his friends, and the Lord gave Job twice as much as he had before" (Job. 42:10).*

As he prayed for his friends, Job was not just restored to the same level of wealth and blessing that he used to have. Job received a double portion of God's abundance and wealth. I am personally convinced that *"the pointing of the finger and speaking of wickedness"* is the main reason why the body of Christ has been powerless in the ministry of restoration. It is the reason that we have seen very little restoration and healing of our wounded brothers and sisters in Christ. But I am also convinced that this will change. As we are conformed into the image of Christ and the church grows into the fullness of Christ, the anointing and grace to restore the fallen and heal the brokenhearted will come back to the church in a very powerful way. For that to happen, we need to repent from critical and judgmental attitudes and words. When we do that, we will receive the restoration and abundance of heaven!

The Two Voices in the Heavenlies

In the beginning of this chapter, we saw that a big part of Jesus' present-day ministry is to be our heavenly intercessor, who lives to pray and intercede for us (Rom. 8:34, Hebr. 7:25). That means that he is pleading for us right now and pleading for our case in the heavenly courts. Jesus is our lawyer and He always speaks in our defense. But there is also another voice that always wants to accuse and criticize us. That is the voice of Satan, our accuser and enemy. The book of revelation speaks about him in the following way: *"… for the accuser of our brethren is cast down, which accused them before our God day and night. And they overcame him by the blood of the Lamb, and by the word of their testimony; and they loved not their lives unto the death"* (Rev. 12:10-11). Satan is the accuser of the brethren and just like Jesus always lives to intercede for us, Satan lives to accuse us day and night. Because of the blood of Jesus, all his accusations against us have been silenced and nullified. Satan no longer has any right to accuse the people of God but he does it anyway. He wants to lie and deceive us into believing that his accusations still are valid.

Partnering with the Right Spirit

This is the reason why criticism is such a big deal to God. Having a critical heart toward other believers and to live with an attitude of accusation against them, is to partner with the devil. If we give voice to our criticism and accusations against other believers, we are releasing spiritual oppression upon the body of Christ by the words we speak. Our words are powerful and have the potential to release both death and life over people. It is for this reason that healing and restoration is lacking in the body of Christ.

To change that, we need to remove "the pointing of the fingers" from our midst and start to partner with Jesus by interceding and praying for the body of Christ. As we allow the love of the Father to penetrate our heart in a deeper way, our hearts will become Christlike. As we have seen, that means that we will have a heart to pray for the body of Christ until we are walking in the fullness of everything God has planned for us.

Prayer that Brings Restoration

In his epistle, James writes that we are to confess our sins to one another and to pray for one another to get healed. *"Confess your faults one to another, and pray one for another, that ye may be healed.*

The effectual fervent prayer of a righteous man availeth much" (Jam. 5:16). I have benefited from practicing this Scripture many times. There have been situations where I have committed sins, and as a result ended up wounded and broken. When I have spoken to a friend or a counselor about it, confessing and repenting from my sin, they have prayed for me and I have been healed. There have also been times when I have waited longer than I should to ask for prayer. That prolonged my pain and the heartache in my soul. Sometimes, we need someone else's prayer to bring healing and restoration when we have fallen into sin. This is especially true if we are stuck in a habitual sin. It is very hard to break these bondages by ourselves, but as our friends stand with us in prayer breakthrough will manifest and we will be healed and delivered. It is a wonderful thing to have people standing with us in prayer. We find many examples of how a praying person can release the will of God in powerful ways. We're going to look at some very good examples in the next chapter.

CHAPTER 12: THE LIFESTYLE & FRUIT OF INTERCESSION

We will continue our study of prayer and intercession by looking at some of biblical examples of intercessors. I find these examples extremely inspiring. We will then look at the fruit of intercession. In the previous chapter we defined the heart of intercession, but it is very helpful to find examples of people who model biblical truths with their lives. In this chapter, we're going to study some of them. They show us how we can partner with Jesus in prayer to see the will of God released in the earth.

Epaphras – Intercessor & Church Planter

Jesus is our foremost example on a life of prayer and intercession, but there is a man by the name of Epaphras, who has always been a personal hero for me in this area. Paul writes these words about this man of prayer:

Epaphras, who is one of your own, a bond-servant of Christ Jesus, sends you his greetings, always striving earnestly for you in his prayers, that you may stand mature and fully assured in all the will of God. I testify for him that he has a deep concern for you and for those who are in Laodicea and Hierapolis" (Col. 4:12-13 NASB).

There is not much information about Epaphras in the Bible, but we know that he was very instrumental in planting the church in Colossae and that he was discipling the believers there (Col. 1:7). Later he also became a fellow prisoner together with the apostle Paul (Philemon 1:23). What we do know is that Epaphras was an intercessor, and that he models powerfully how intercession and prayer flows from a Christlike heart.

His heart had been transformed by intimacy with Jesus and the love of the Father. Because of this, Epaphras shared the burden of Jesus for His church. This compelled him to contend in fervent prayer for the saints in Colossae to grow into the image of Christ. Intercession always flows from a Christlike heart. As the love of Christ continues to work within us, we will share His burden for a mature bride. The only possible response to sharing His burden is to give ourselves to a lifestyle of intercession and prayer.

Biblical Examples of Intercessors

There are many other good examples of intercessors and prayer warriors in the Bible. Even though our space is too limited here to study their lives in detail, I want to mention some of them. As you read through this list, I recommend that you take some time to meditate and pray over the life stories of these heroes of faith. There is a lot of insight to draw from their stories and experiences with God:

- **Abraham** pleaded with God not to let judgement come upon Sodom and Gomorrah, but above all he asked God to save the righteous inhabitants of these cities from the coming judgement. Even though these cities were ruined and destroyed, we still see how Abraham had the heart of a true intercessor (Gen. 18:20-33).

- **Moses** carried the people of Israel in prayer through the forty years in the wilderness. The prayers and fervent intercession of Moses compelled God to relent, change His mind and show mercy to Israel (Exod. 17:8-13, 32:11-14, 30-33, Num. 14:11-20, Deut. 9:13-18).

- **Hanna** was a barren woman, but through prayer and intercession she conceived and gave birth to a son. That son was the great prophet, Samuel. Her prayers birthed his prophetic ministry. That ministry touched the whole nation of Israel, causing the people of God to once again be able to hear the word of the Lord (1 Sam. 1:1-28).

- **Samuel** prayed for the people of God all his life since he was a young boy. The Prophet Samuel would consider it a sin to stop praying for them (1 Sam. 12:23).

- **Elijah** prayed and no rain fell in Israel for three and a half years, but then he prayed again and rain started to fall almost immediately. James underscores that Elijah the prophet was a man just like us. But there is power in the fervent prayer of a righteous man (1 Kings 18:41-46, Jam. 5:16-18).

- **Huldah the Prophetess** prayed and prophesied to king Josiah about his destiny, and the soon coming exile of the people of Judah (2 Chron. 34:20-28).

- **Ezra** interceded and represented the people of God in prayer of repentance, which led to the people repenting from mixed marriages with the gentiles (Ezra 9:6-15).

- **Nehemiah** prayed for the restoration of the people of God and for the city of Jerusalem. He asked God for favor in his plan to return to Jerusalem and lead the work of restoration. As a result, Nehemiah was operating in a powerful ministry of restoration (Neh. 1:1-11).

- **Job** prayed for his friends and as he prayed, he himself was restored and blessed as well (Job. 42:10).

- **Daniel** gave himself to prayer and intercession with fasting for the prophetic promises given by Jeremiah to be fulfilled. (Dan. 9:1-19).

- **Anna** served God with prayer and fasting day and night in the temple (Luke 2:36-37).

- **The apostle Paul** prayed for the churches that he had planted, as well as the churches that had been planted by his friends. You can find some of Paul's prayers in his letters (Eph. 1:16-19, 3:14-20, Phil. 1:9-11, Col. 1:9-12).

There are many powerful examples of intercessors in the Bible, but I wanted to include this list as a resource for further study on the ministry of intercession. The history of the people of God has been shaped by people who have served Him with their prayers and fervent intercession. In the New Testament, we find several examples of this. The apostle Paul asked the churches to pray for him on several occasions.

Intercession Brings Boldness & Wisdom to Our Preaching

In Ephesians, Paul instructs us to be *"…praying always with all prayer and supplication in the Spirit, and watching thereunto with all perseverance and supplication for all saints" (Eph. 6:18)*. The apostle Paul encourages us to pray with all prayers. These different types of prayer would include some of the spiritual disciplines that we are studying in this book. For example, worship, soaking, fasting, and intercession are included in all kinds of prayers. We need to have a life with Jesus that is rich in all different expressions of prayer. Intercession is among these expressions.

Paul continues by asking for personal prayer and as he does, he reveals a powerful principle. He wanted the believers in Ephesus to pray for all the saints, but also *"… for me, that utterance may be given unto me, that I may open my mouth boldly, to make known the mystery of the gospel, for which I am an ambassador in bonds: that therein I may speak boldly, as I ought to speak" (Eph. 6:19-20)*. Paul understood that their intercession would impart more boldness and wisdom from heaven, which would make his ministry even more fruitful and effective. When we are praying and for our missionaries and evangelists, Jesus will impart His boldness and wisdom and, which will make the preaching of the gospel much more effective and powerful (Col. 4:2-4, 2 Tess. 3:1).

Prayer for Boldness & Miracles During Persecution

This is the kind of prayer that the church in Jerusalem prayed in response to the persecution from the religious leaders within the city:

And now, Lord, look at their threats, and grant it to Your bond-servants to speak Your word with all confidence, while You extend Your hand to heal, and signs and wonders take place through the name of Your holy Servant Jesus (Acts 4:29-30 NASB).

They didn't respond by praying defensive prayers, asking God to put an end the persecution. They prayed for the boldness to preach more effectively and that the Father would release more signs and wonders. By the response they received, we can be sure that the Father likes bold prayers of this kind. *"And when they had prayed, the place where they had gathered together was shaken, and they were all filled with the Holy Spirit and began to speak the word of God with boldness"* (Acts 4:31 NASB). Today some people get nervous as we pray for people and they begin to shake under the power of God. But here, the whole building began to shake as the Father poured out a greater measure of the power and anointing of the Holy Spirit upon His children!

Praying for Kings & People in Authority

We are called to live in peace and quietness. For that to happen, we need to have wise people leading our nations. Paul therefore encourages us with the following words: *"I urge, then, first of all, that petitions, prayers, intercession and thanksgiving be made for all people— for kings and all those in authority, that we may live peaceful and quiet lives in all godliness and holiness. This is good, and pleases God our Savior"* (1 Tim. 2:1-3 NIV). It is important to realize that sitting at home complaining about the wrong decisions that our government makes will not change things to the better. In fact, it will make it worse. We have already seen that having a critical heart means that we are partnering with the wrong spirit. We can make a difference in the world by interceding for the leaders and government of the nations. When we do that, God will work on them and release His wisdom into the heart of our leaders and politicians. I want to encourage you to set aside time to pray for the leaders of your nation, as well as other political leaders in the world. As the body of Christ, we can have a powerful influence on the decision of leaders and rulers by praying and interceding for them.

Intercession that Brings Fruitfulness & Joy

In my other books, I have shared rather extensively on how Jesus have called us to live fruitful lives that bring lasting results. This fruitfulness is connected to our intercession. *"Ye have not chosen me, but I have chosen you, and ordained you, that ye should go and bring forth fruit, and that your fruit should remain: that whatsoever ye shall ask of the Father in my name, he may give it you"* (John 15:16). It is because Jesus has decided that we should bear remaining fruit that the Father will give us whatever we ask for. The way that we become fruitful is by praying. This is how the Father gives us the fruit that Jesus has promised. Yet, there is a lot of believers who don't see remaining fruit in their life. This is because bearing fruit does not happen automatically. As we partner with God in prayer the fruit will manifest in our lives. We should always pray big and bold prayers, because those are the prayers that release rich fruit that remains. A little later Jesus makes the following statement:

"And on that day you will not question Me about anything. Truly, truly I say to you, if you ask the Father for anything in My name, He will give it to you. Until now you have asked for nothing in My name; ask and you will receive, so that your joy may be made full" (John 16:23-24 NASB). Answered prayers causes us to bear fruit, but they will cause our joy to be made full as well. By living a life of fervent prayer and intercession, we bear fruit that remains and can live in the fullness of joy.

Persistent Faith & Prayer

"Then Jesus told his disciples a parable to show them that they should always pray and not give up" (Luke 18:1 NIV). It is important to Jesus that we learn how to pray with endurance, because we are not always seeing the results we want as quickly as we expected. These are the times when we might become tempted to give up. To illustrate why we should keep praying with persistent faith, Jesus shares a parable about a woman who kept coming to the judge to plead her case for justice and legal protection (Luke 18:2-6). This judge did not fear God, and he had no regard or respect for people. At first, he was unwilling to help her, but because she persisted, he finally gave in, realizing that she would never stop pleading her case. He granted this woman the justice and legal protection that she needed. Then Jesus continues: *"And will not God bring about justice for his chosen ones, who cry out to him day and night? Will he keep putting them off? I tell you, he will see that they get justice, and quickly. However, when the Son of Man comes, will he find faith on the earth"* (Luke 18:7-8 NIV). Just like Jesus always lives to intercede for us, we who are His chosen ones can cry out to Him day and night. Our persistent prayer will be answered and we will get justice quickly. From the Father's perspective, getting justice means that we receive all the blessings that Jesus has won for us on the cross. Jesus finished this statement by asking if the Son of Man would find such persistent faith on the earth? My answer is: Yes! Jesus will find such great faith in our

hearts. Let's cultivate a lifestyle of prayer and intercession that releases the love of the Father all over the world!

Prayer & Faith

We have looked at the importance of being persistent in prayer. Yet, we have probably all met people who have been very fervent and persistent in their prayer life for many years, but still have not seen a much result. Persistence is not enough. Jesus is looking for persistence combined with bold faith. *"But without faith it is impossible to please him: for he that cometh to God must believe that he is, and that he is a rewarder of them that diligently seek him"* (Hebr. 11:6). Our faith pleases God and when we seek Him diligently, He will always reward our faith. It is important to remember that *"faith is the substance of things hoped for, the evidence of things not seen"* (Hebr. 11:1). Faith is always based on the promises of God, and the blessings that we have been given in Christ. It is faith that gives us boldness in our prayer. Jesus reveals how powerful it is to pray in faith by the following statement: *"Therefore I say unto you, What things soever ye desire, when ye pray, believe that ye receive them, and ye shall have them"* (Mark 11:24). To know all the privileges and blessings we have in Christ, we need revelation. When the Holy Spirit enlightens our heart, faith will come so that our prayers will be answered.

Birthing New Vision and Breakthroughs in Prayer

A lot of the results we see in our ministry today is the result of our prayer and intercession. I remember when I used to work as a pastor in a church, located in a small village up in the mountain areas of Sweden. At that time, I felt such a burden for all the pain, brokenness, and unhealed wounds in the body of Christ. I stayed for days at a time in my office to pray for a breakthrough in our inner healing ministry. I only went back home to sleep and the rest of the day I prayed and interceded to see the body of Christ restored. I am convinced that a lot of the fruit that we see today in our ministry of healing and restoration, is a result of the work we did in prayer all those years ago. The interesting thing is that this never felt like a legalistic burden to us, probably because our intercession was fueled by the love of the Father. We had deep desire to see more healing and restoration happening in the body of Christ. I could give many more examples, but something even better is for you to start praying and get some more testimonies yourself! It is such a wonderful joy to co-labor with the Father in intercession by birthing visions and releasing the Kingdom.

Cultivating a Lifestyle of Prayer & Intercession

A lifestyle of prayer and intercession guarantees that we will live very exciting lives. We can have a huge impact on the world and the body of Christ through our prayer and intercession. Here are some ways through which we can grow in our prayer life:

1. **Knowing the Heart of Jesus.**
   All prayer and intercession begin with aligning our heart with Jesus, so that He can share His desires and passions with us. The thing that Jesus desires, more than anything else is a restored and mature bride for Himself. As we share in His desire, we will pray and intercede until all of Gods plans and promises for us are fulfilled. As His love increasingly fills our hearts, prayer and intercession is born within our spirits as a response to His love.

2. **Listen to and Follow the Leading of the Holy Spirit.**
   In the previous chapter, we saw that none of us knows how to pray very well, but the Holy Spirit helps us to pray by interceding through us. We should expect the Holy Spirit's guidance and leading as we pray. When He leads us to intercede in a certain direction we should

always go with the flow and pray for whatever He leads. That will turn intercession into an adventure every time!

3. **Turning Criticism into Intercession.**
When I notice that I have a critical and judgmental heart toward someone, I have developed a habit of spending some extra time to pray for them. I ask the Holy Spirit to reveal their calling and identity, so that I can see them through the eyes of the Father. That has given me a more constructive way to deal with criticism and it has also cleansed my heart from a lot of judgmental and critical attitudes. I noticed that I am less critical towards people now, and much faster to pray for them. There is so much joy in being able to stand together with people in prayer.

4. **Loving the Body of Christ.**
We need to develop the same heart of love and passion for the body of Christ that Jesus Himself has. As I have been growing in love and compassion for the body of Christ, I have been praying much more than ever for the church to reach full maturity in Christ.

5. **Living with a Vision of a Healed and Restored Church.**
I have intentionally studied the Bible, read many books, and listened to a lot of teaching, concerning the healing and restoration of the body of Christ. The reason for this is that I wanted to get a vision of how the church, when having been raised up and fully matured, will look like. As I have gotten a bigger vision of a restored church, and how far we are from there, my prayers for the church to be fully restored, have become much more fervent than ever. I am convinced that we will see a fully restored and glorious church in the earth before Jesus comes back! In the chapter on mission and later in this book, I address intercession in connection to the harvest and the sending

out of laborers to the mission field, but here I wanted to focus on praying and interceding for the bride of Christ.

CHAPTER 13: WORDS THAT IMPART GRACE

In order to partner with the love of the Father, we need to build habits that bring healing and freedom to the world. One way in which we can do that is through our words. Jesus promised that the faith-filled words we speak will move mountains:

Have faith in God. For verily I say unto you, that whosoever shall say unto this mountain, be thou removed, and be thou cast into the sea; and shall not doubt in his heart, but shall believe that those things which he saith shall come to pass; he shall have whatsoever he saith (Mark 11: 22-23).

Words are very powerful. God created the universe through His spoken word and all the way throughout the Bible we read about *"… God, who quickeneth the dead, and calleth those things which be not as though they were" (Rom. 4:17).* Since we have been created in the image of God, our words are more than just means through which we communicate. Our words carry spiritual power that can even move mountains.

Jesus told us that we will have whatever we say when we declare things from a believing heart. As we speak, we need to be aware that our words have the potential to build up and impart grace to the people listening (Eph. 4:29). We have been given the ability to release life or death over people and situations, through our spoken words. By speaking the Word of God in faith, we release the power of God to heal, deliver and restore in a powerful way. Therefore, we need to make a choice to speak the truth in love, always with the goal to redeem and reveal the heart of the Father.

Faith and Words

This doesn't mean that everything we're speaking and declaring will happen automatically. All of us have made declarations that were in line with the promises of God, but still they didn't come to pass. It is the confession from a believing heart that releases the power of God. Paul writes "... *that if thou shalt confess with thy mouth the Lord Jesus, and shalt believe in thine heart that God hath raised him from the dead, thou shalt be saved. For with the heart man believeth unto righteousness; and with the mouth confession is made unto salvation" (Rom 10:8-10).* We get saved by believing in our hearts unto righteousness, and by declaring what we believe by confessing Jesus as Lord. This is how our words release creative power. When we declare what we believe in our hearts, we will have whatever we say. This is the spirit of faith. *"We having the same spirit of faith, according as it is written, I believed, and therefore have I spoken; we also believe, and therefore speak" (2 Cor. 4:13).* Faith is released through words, and faith is always born in our hearts. This leads us back to an important principle: *All of God's dealings with us, always begin with the heart.*

Faith Begins within our Hearts

True faith is always built on revelation from the Holy Spirit. We can't create faith, but faith is born through our relationship with God. As the Holy Spirit reveals the Word of God to us, our heart is enlightened and we can see what God sees (Eph. 1:17-19). That is how we receive revelation from God, and faith is always built on revelation. *"So then faith cometh by hearing, and hearing by the word of God" (Rom. 10:17).* As we hear and read the Word of God, faith is born within our hearts. When we speak according to our faith, the power of God is released through our words. This is not magic. We can't create our own reality by affirmations.

We are always dependent on the revelation that Jesus gives. The reason that some people have misunderstood this teaching, and as a result misapplied it, is because it has been disconnected from intimacy with God. That will lead to legalism and futile attempts of trying to convince ourselves of things that we are not in reality believing. But as we speak according to what we see in the heart of the Father, powerful things will happen!

Learn to Encourage Yourself in the Lord

We can encourage and strengthen our inner man by speaking the promises of the Father over our lives. David did this a lot. He had learnt to speak to his soul. *"Why are you in despair, O my soul? And why have you become restless and disturbed within me? Hope in God and wait expectantly for Him, for I shall again praise Him for the help of His presence"* (Ps. 42:5 AMP see also Ps. 43:5). This was the way David encouraged himself in God (1 Sam. 30:6). We can't rely on other people to be there for us with an encouraging word. There might come bad days when we find ourselves both discouraged and heartbroken.

The good news is that we can always encourage ourselves in the Lord. In the psalm above, we see an example of David telling his soul to praise the Lord. David did that to remind himself that his help came from God. Here is another passage where king David reminded himself to bless the Lord and remember the goodness of God. He wrote this psalm: *"Bless the LORD, O my soul: And all that is within me, bless his holy name. Bless the LORD, O my soul, and forget not all his benefits"* (Ps. 103:1-2). We need to follow David's example and remind ourselves of the goodness of God regularly. When we're facing problems in life, or when we must deal with difficult situations and people, it is easy to forget the goodness of God. But it is by knowing the heart of the Father that we find strength in tough situations.

We need to remind ourselves of the miracles and breakthroughs that God has done for us. David continues by recounting his own experiences of the goodness and love of the Lord: *"Who forgiveth all thine iniquities; who healeth all thy diseases; who redeemeth thy life from destruction; who crowneth thee with lovingkindness and tender mercies; who satisfieth thy mouth with good things; So that thy youth is renewed like the eagle's" (Ps. 103:3-5).* We can speak to our soul by praising God for all the miracles we have seen and thank Him for the blessings we have received.

My Experience of Prophetic Declarations

I have made it my habit to encourage myself in the Lord every morning. Whenever the Holy Spirit shows more of His plans, I write down what He reveals to me as a prophetic declaration. I have made a list of these declarations and I like to begin my days by proclaiming them over my life. I have seen a lot of exciting things being released because of this. In fact, this is how I began writing books. For many years I received a lot of prophetic words about writing. I knew that it was the Holy Spirit speaking. My problem was that writing had always been a struggle for me; I just couldn't get it done. I had tried a couple of times, but always ended up in despair, usually before even finishing the first page. Writing a whole book felt totally impossible, but the Holy Spirit kept speaking to me about it. Finally, hope started to grow in my heart and I accepted that one day I would write a book.

I wrote a declaration of faith about writing books that reveals the heart of the Father. I started to speak this declaration over my life every day. Over time, there was a shift in my spirit and I started to tap into the anointing of writing and I jumped into the flow of the Holy Spirit. Now I have written two books already, and this is now my third one. A couple of years ago, this wouldn't have been possible, but declarations of faith have the power to move mountains!

Restraining our Speech

Since our words carries so much power and authority, we must learn how to discipline our tongue. The more we learn to control our speech, the less problems we will have. Since I love to talk to people, and my ministry revolves a lot around communication, this has become an important issue for me. James seems to agree with me. He has a lot to say about the potential damage that our undisciplined tongue can cause. It can harm both ourselves and other people. James compares our tongue with a destructive fire: *"And the tongue is a fire, the very world of unrighteousness; the tongue is set among our body's parts as that which defiles the whole body and sets on fire the course of our life, and is set on fire by hell"* (Jam. 3:6 NASB). In fact, our speech can contaminate our life and defile the people that listen. Because of this, Jesus was speaking of words making us unclean (Matt. 15:11). It is impossible for us to deal with this issue in our own strength. *"For every species of beasts and birds, of reptiles and creatures of the sea, is tamed and has been tamed by the human race. But no one among mankind can tame the tongue; it is a restless evil, full of deadly poison"* (Jam. 6:7-8 NASB).

We need help to control our tongue, but the good news is that we are not left on our own in this endeavor. Jesus lives within us, and He wants to express His own life through us. That involves the way we speak. When we surrender to Jesus and allow Him to work with us, we will grow in the fruit of the Spirit called self-control (Gal. 5:22-23). Jesus wants to help us to tame our tongue, so that we can speak words that both build up and impart grace.

Tongues of Fire

As we just read, James compares our tongue to a fire. That is no coincidence. At the day of Pentecost, when the Holy Spirit was being poured out upon God's children, tongues of fire appeared as a prophetic sign upon their heads. *"And tongues that looked like fire appeared to them, distributing themselves, and a tongue rested on each one of them. And they were all filled with the Holy Spirit and began to speak with different tongues, as the Spirit was giving them the ability to speak out"* (Acts 2:3-4 NASB).Our speech will change as we are being filled with the Holy Spirit. This is one of the reasons why speaking in tongues is such a blessing. The Holy Spirit uses tongues to discipline our speech. It is significant that the disciples began to speak in tongues as soon as they were filled with the Holy Spirit. As our words are filled with the life and presence of God, miracles will be released through our declarations of faith.

Isaiah's Encounter with the Lord

Usually, one of the first things that happens as we spend time in the presence of God, is that we become convicted of our unclean speech. Isaiah had an experience that reveals how this works. In a vision, he saw the Lord seated on His throne. As this happened, he almost instantly came under heavy conviction from the Holy Spirit: *"Then I said, "Woe to me, for I am ruined! Because I am a man of unclean lips, And I live among a people of unclean lips; For my eyes have seen the King, the Lord of armies"* (Isa. 6:5 NASB). When Isaiah received this vision, he was already functioning in his prophetic ministry. Yet, he was still struggling with his unclean speech and when he encountered God, he was quickly convicted about this.

The good news is that true conviction always leads to repentance and a greater level of purity. True conviction from the Lord never leaves us in condemnation but leads us to Jesus who sets us free. God already has a solution for our mess: *"Then one of the seraphim flew to me with a burning coal in his hand, which he had taken from the altar with tongs. He touched my mouth with it and said, "Behold, this has touched your lips; and your guilt is taken away and atonement is made for your sin"* (Isa. 6:6-7 NASB). Isaiah was cleansed from his unclean speech, so that he could minister to God's people with a clear message of repentance and healing. With this breakthrough came a new boldness and longing to respond to God's call. Isaiah immediately answered the Lord's calling: *"Then I heard the voice of the Lord, saying, "Whom shall I send, and who will go for Us?" Then I said, "Here am I. Send me" (Isa. 6:8)!* Cleansing always leads to an eager longing to serve God more.

Cleansed by the Blood of Jesus

Just like the prophet Isaiah, we need to be cleansed from unclean lips from time to time. The good news is that we are living in the New Covenant and we have already received a total forgiveness through the blood of Jesus. Since His blood washes us, we can be cleansed continually. As Jesus baptizes us in the Holy Spirit and fire, our speech will be more purified and our words will become empowered by the anointing of the Holy Spirit. Like Isaiah, we will be filled with boldness, so that we can answer the holy call to preach the gospel of Christ. Our purity and boldness come from the finished work of Jesus and the fire of the Holy Spirit. As we're speaking His Word, miracles will happen and people will be transformed by the love of God!

Words that Build Up and Impart Grace Others

We always impart something to other people as we're speaking, and it is important that we are aware of that. For this reason, Paul wrote to the church at Ephesus: *"Let no corrupt word proceed out of your mouth, but what is good for necessary edification, that it may impart grace to the hearers" (Eph. 4:29 NKJV).* We always speak out of the abundance from our hearts (Matt 12:34). What we have in our hearts will sooner or later come out, which is one of the big reasons it is such a blessing that the love of God has been poured into our hearts through the Holy Spirit (Rom 5:5). As we abide in His love, the words we speak are fueled by His grace. This is how we can adhere to this exhortation by Paul: *"Let your conversation be gracious and attractive so that you will have the right response for everyone" (Col. 4:6 NLT)*. This type of speech will impart His love to those who listen. This is what the Bible calls the words of the wise. Throughout the rest of this chapter, we're going to look at some of the components of possessing a wise tongue.

Speaking Words that Bring Life

We have the power to impart both life, as well as death through our words. *"Wise words satisfy like a good meal; the right words bring satisfaction. The tongue can bring death or life; those who love to talk will reap the consequences" (Prov. 18:20-21 NLT)*. Some of my most painful experiences is connected to people who spoke words of death into my life. On the other hand, some of the memories that I cherish the most are certainly connected to people encouraging me by speaking words that imparted life to me.

It is both a wonderful possibility and a big responsibility to know that our words carry that much authority. Those of us who like to talk need to be aware of the consequences of what we say. We need to realize that there will always be a harvest from the words we have spoken. Our words are like seeds and we need to learn to speak in a way that gives us the harvest we desire. We have seen earlier in this book that the words of Jesus Christ impart life and spiritual substance when received in an open heart. As we're allowing the love of the Father to shape our speech, our words will have the same effect, since Jesus will speak through us.

Words of Healing

It has been very interesting to study the book of Proverbs on the topic of our words and speech. It provides a lot of insight on how wise people speak, in comparison to the words of a fool. Here is one example: *"Reckless words are like the thrusts of a sword, cutting remarks meant to stab and to hurt. But the words of the wise soothe and heal" (Prov. 12:18 TPT)*. Wise words can bring healing to a broken heart and provide comfort to people in pain. Words that minister healing is a fruit that comes from the tree of life. *"When you speak healing words, you offer others fruit from the tree of life. But unhealthy, negative words do nothing but crush their hopes"* (Prov. 15:4 TPT). If we create an atmosphere where we speak healing and life to one another, we will build a culture of creativity and courage. That is how Jesus speaks. He always imparts wisdom and hope. If we're criticizing and speaking negatively, we crush people's hope and courage. That is the language of the devil, who is an accuser that constantly wants to remind us of our shortcomings to discourage us and force us to give up. As believers, we are called to speak words of healing and hope that encourage and bring restoration. That type of speech is very attractive because it is the language of heaven. *"Nothing is more appealing than speaking beautiful, life-giving words. For they release sweetness to our souls and inner healing to our spirits"* (Prov 16:24 TPT).

Soft and Well-timed Words

Another characteristic of wise speech is that it consists of words, which are spoken in a well-timed and soft way. *"A soft answer turns away wrath, but a harsh word stirs up anger. The tongue of the wise uses knowledge rightly, but the mouth of fools pours forth foolishness"* (Prov. 15:1-2 NKJV). Our culture has become a culture driven by anger. By observing how people communicate with one another, both in real life and online, we can observe that the words spoken are often harsh and hurtful, but also spoken in a very demeaning way. That type of communication is one of the hallmarks of foolish speaking.

We have many opportunities to bring reconciliation from Jesus by responding with soft, well-timed words that turn away wrath and minister healing. Responding with a soft answer is not only about how we speak, but also about good timing. *"A man hath joy by the answer of his mouth: And a word spoken in due season, how good is it" (Prov. 15:23)*! We need to be sure that the people we are speaking to are ready to hear our input as we speak. This is about knowing the right timing to give an answer. Proverbs compares this skill to a work of art: *"A word fitly spoken is like apples of gold in pictures of silver. As an earring of gold, and an ornament of fine gold, so is a wise reprover upon an obedient ear" (Prov. 25:11-12)*. The Holy Spirit is a master at this skill. He knows exactly how to get through to our heart. He wants to help us discipline our speech, so that our words align with the words of Jesus. Then our words will bring healing and restoration to many broken hearts.

A Christ-Centered Speech

Cultivating wise speech always begin in our hearts. Whatever we allow to grow in our hearts, will come out in our speech. This is the reason that Paul encourages us to: *"Let the word of Christ dwell in you richly in all wisdom; teaching and admonishing one another in psalms and hymns and spiritual songs, singing with grace in your hearts to the Lord" (Col. 3:16)*. As we keep filling our lives with the gospel, our hearts will be filled until it overflows with the good news of Jesus Christ. That will manifest in the way we speak.

The truly wise person centers his or her speech around the good news of Jesus Christ. When Paul writes that we are to teach one another in psalms, hymns and spiritual songs, he is not telling us to walk around singing all the time. What Paul is saying is that when our speech is filled with the words of Christ, it becomes a form of worship that both edifies people and glorifies God. We have a wonderful opportunity to partner with the love of Christ by allowing the word of Christ, the gospel, to dwell richly among us. Since the gospel is the power of God, this type of speech will release freedom, healing, and salvation to the world.

Jesus is the High Priest of Our Confession

All of heaven will back us up when we confess and declare the promises of God over our lives, families and calling. This is a part of the present-day ministry of Jesus, as our glorious High Priest. *"Therefore, holy brethren, partakers of the heavenly calling, consider the Apostle and High Priest of our confession, Christ Jesus" (Hebr. 3:1 NKJV).* As we're speaking and declaring His promises in faith, Jesus brings our confession before the Father to release the power of God on our behalf. I love this truth! It is a privilege to partner with the love of the Father by releasing His life into this world. By proclaiming the Word of God, we're building up our brothers and sisters in Christ, but we are also transforming the world by releasing salvation and freedom into the earth.

Learning to Speak Life and Healing

Surrendering our tongue to God is an area where we all need to grow. I'm convinced that I need to grow in this area more than most people. Still, there are a few principles that have helped me along the way, and I would like to share them with you below:

1. **Let the Word of Christ Dwell Richly within your Heart.** Since what we allow into our heart always come out, our speech is always a matter of the heart. What we allow to dwell within us will one day become our life. Therefore, we should make sure that we listen to the gospel all the time, so that our hearts stays filled with the good news of Jesus Christ.

2. **Surrender your Tongue and Speech to the Holy Spirit.** We have already seen that we cannot tame our tongue by ourselves, but we can invite the Holy Spirit to help us. He is a gentleman and He will not push His will upon us. But as we invite Him to work on our speech, He will

surely help us. As He does that, the fruit of the Spirit will grow and become more visible through our speech. This will cause our words to release the life of Christ, and to be filled with the anointing of the Holy Spirit.

3. **Listen to People Who Speak Life.**
   I have discovered the blessing of surrounding myself with people who speaks words that are full of grace, life, and faith. This way of speaking comes from a revelation of the gospel. I actively seek for these kinds of voices. I follow their social medias, I listen to their podcasts and read their books. We need to be very intentional with the voices we allow to influence our lives. I recommend that you surround yourself with the people who speak life by glorifying Jesus. Their way of speaking will eventually rub off on you.

4 . **Stay Away from Foolish Speech.**
   Many people seem to be unaware of how much they are being influenced by the speech and attitudes from the people they are listening to. I always unfollow people on social media who speak bad about churches and leaders, or if someone is always just posting negative stuff. Even if it would turn out to be true, I don't need to know about ministries and churches that I am not responsible for. I am careful not to allow friends into my inner circle that speak or write a lot of negative stuff. This attitude tends to spread, and I want to stay focused on the good news of Jesus Christ.

5. **Practice Speaking Words of Faith.**
   When I got saved and started to hear teaching about the power of words, I realized that through my broken past, I had been taught to speak very negatively. I had a very hard time breaking that habit. To build a good habit of

speaking more positively and faith-filled words, I wrote down a list of declarations of faith that I began to declare over my life every morning. That habit has been sticking with me ever since, I'm still declaring God's promises over my life every morning. I recommend that you adopt a similar habit to create new ways of speaking.

CHAPTER 14: DREAMING WITH GOD

The Father has a lot of big dreams and plans for us. He wants us to partner with Him by being a people who disciple nations and advance His Kingdom all over the earth. Our heavenly Father is a visionary and a dreamer. Since we are His own children, being dreamers and visionaries is written into our new creation DNA. This is one of the ways in which we can partner with the love of the Father. God speaks to us through dreams and visions. In fact, dreaming with God and living with a vision is a direct result of being filled with the Holy Spirit.

And it shall be in the last days, God says, That I will pour out My Spirit on all mankind; And your sons and your daughters will prophesy, and your young men will see visions, and your old men will have dreams; And even on My male and female servants I will pour out My Spirit in those days, and they will prophesy (Acts 2:17-18 NASB).

This is important for us to understand because I have spoken to so many believers who wait for God to speak to them. But since they have a hard time believing that their dreams and visions are from God, they don't dare to follow their dreams. Yet, dreams and visions are one of the most important and common ways in which the Holy Spirit speaks to us. I consider being able to follow and fulfill my dreams as one of the Father's most precious gifts to me. This gift is a huge expression of the Father's love for us, and fulfilling our dreams and visions is a big part of being free in Christ.

Created to Dream Big

Since we have a Father who dream big and we have been created in His image, we are called to do likewise. Our dreams should never be limited, either by our circumstances or natural gifts. Not even what seems to be possible for us is an issue. The greatness of our dreams and visions can only be limited by the greatness of God. That means that all things are possible. A common sign that we have a dream or vision that is from God, is that it seems impossible for us to accomplish in the natural. *"With men this is impossible; but with God all things are possible" (Matt. 19:26).* I have learned that it doesn't matter how big prayers I pray or even how much I expect God to do, He always supersedes my expectations.

Our Father has a big heart for us, and He loves to surprise us by doing more with our dreams and visions than we could think or even imagine. *"Now unto him that is able to do exceeding abundantly above all that we ask or think, according to the power that worketh in us" (Eph. 3:20).* So, I challenge you to dare to dream big and pray big prayers. As you do that, you will be surprised by the way in which our Father will shower you in His goodness and grace and how your dreams and visions will be fulfilled in a much greater way than you had ever imagined!

Renewing our Minds to Think Bigger

For us to be able to receive the dreams and visions of God for our lives, we need to be renewed in our thinking. Paul encourages us to *"… not conform to the pattern of this world, but be transformed by the renewing of your mind. Then you will be able to test and approve what God's will is—his good, pleasing and perfect will" (Rom. 12:2 NIV).* One of the patterns of this world is to think realistically and be "wise" in our approach to life, but this is a worldly wisdom. God wants us to be realistic according to His perspective, which means knowing that all things are possible. God will fulfill all the dreams He has given to us way beyond our wildest dreams. His power is at work, both in and through us! When our minds are renewed, we will be able to think creatively and we will become possibility thinkers because God is with us.

The Importance of Spiritual Sight

We need to have spiritual sight to know where we are going. God provides such sight by unveiling His plans to us through dreams and visions. These contain our calling and purpose in the form of a small seed. When these dreams are planted in the soil of our hearts and we nourish and water them, they will grow until they become our reality. When God speaks to us, we should follow Mary's example and keep the words we have received in our hearts and think about them often (Luke 2:19). Spiritual sight is given to us as the Holy Spirit enlightens the eyes of our hearts. *"I pray that the eyes of your heart may be enlightened, so that you will know what is the hope of His calling, what are the riches of the glory of His inheritance in the saints, and what is the boundless greatness of His power toward us who believe" (Eph 1:18-19).* Our inheritance as children of God includes the purpose and destiny of our lives. When the Holy Spirit enlightens our hearts, we will be able to see His vision for our future. As we begin to move in the direction of the vision, we will work towards the fulfilment of our vision one step at a time.

Satan is a Dream Killer

Since the dreams God gives us contain our destiny in seed form, Satan is always out to steal our vision and kill our dreams. It is easier for him to steal a seed than to uproot and pull a whole tree out of our hearts. Therefore, he goes after our dreams. The vision that has been established within our hearts is much harder for him to steal. Satan wants to deceive us into becoming cynical and afraid of dreaming big. He tells us that dreaming to big will lead to disappointment. Satan wants us to be limited by our present circumstances. He wants to deceive us to define our future with God by past disappointments. He is a dream killer, who knows that if he can steal our dreams, he will shut down our future. We need to guard our dreams within our hearts.

Without Vision People Perish

Jesus came to give us overflowing and abundant life (John 10:10). A huge part of being alive in Jesus Christ is to become a Kingdom dreamer and a heavenly visionary. The opposite is true as well. Where there is a lack of life, there is no vision. In the book of Proverbs, we read about a very important principle: *"Where there is no vision, the people perish" (Prov. 29:18).* The devil's strategy is always aimed at stealing our hope and faith for change. He is not interested in our circumstances, our health, or financial situation, but these are still common areas of spiritual attacks. The reason is that he uses these areas to get to our heart, so that he can steal the vision that God has placed there. He knows that if we become disillusioned and cynical, he can steal our calling. *"Hope deferred maketh the heart sick: But when the desire cometh, it is a tree of life" (Prov. 13:12).* Dreams and visions are the language of heaven. In the same way, cynicism and hopelessness is the devil's language. If our hope is crushed, our heart becomes sick. All of us will have to face disappointments and pain, but we must learn how to process and walk through them together with the Holy Spirit.

My Life Changed because of Vision

In my old life, my heart used to be filled with disappointment. I was totally lost in hopelessness and depression before I met Jesus. I even contemplated suicide. I did that because I had no hope for a better future. Those days were painful and filled with anxiety. But when Jesus came into my life this all changed! He brought so much hope and vision with Him. The Holy Spirit started to fill my internal world with dreams of God's future for my life, and as I started the life that the Father was inviting me into, I said yes to that invitation. As I started to dream with Jesus, I prayed and aligned my life with what I saw. I found direction and hope for my future. I slowly realized that I wanted to be alive and to my amazement, I had even fallen in love with the wonderful gift that is called life! In fact, Jesus wants us to enjoy life and embrace all our days as gifts from the Father. It is an amazing privilege to be alive. *"The thief cometh not, but for to steal, and to kill, and to destroy: I am come that they might have life, and that they might have it more abundantly"* (John 10:10).

The Prayer of Jabez

One person who was a huge inspiration for me as the Father gave me a vision of the restored life was a man by the name of Jabez. The Bible describes him like this: *"Jabez was more honorable than his brothers. His mother had named him Jabez, saying, "I gave birth to him in pain"* (1 Chron. 4:9 NIV). Because his mother gave birth to him in great pain, she named him Jabez, which means *"he makes sorrowful"*. In the Bible, names always carry prophetic meaning. When he received the name Jabez, he became destined to be one whose life would cause pain and sorrow. That is a tragic destiny, but the time came when Jabez refused to accept that as his fate. He took hold of his identity and purpose with God in prayer. He had powerful dreams and visions for the future, which is why he dared to pray these prayers. This was his request to the Father: *"Jabez cried out to the God of Israel, "Oh, that you would bless me and enlarge my territory! Let your hand be with me, and keep me from harm so that I will be free from pain." And God granted his request"* (1 Chron. 4:10 NIV).

This is a powerful prayer! It is no coincidence that people have written books and preached many sermons based on this prayer. Our Father has given it to inspire us to believe in the dreams and visions from heaven. When we believe and pray bold prayers, the Father will grant us our request. He will bless us and enlarge our territory. He will be with us, protect us from the enemy and restore us from the pain of our past!

Perceiving Who You Are Becoming

Like Jabez did, I started to see myself as a free and restored man. I refused to accept that I was destined to a life in brokenness and pain. I started to see myself as a good husband, father, preacher, but first and foremost a mature son of God. That gave me hope. It gave me a reason to fight to get there. I started to desire change and I realized that I could partner with the Holy Spirit in making these dreams happening. This is how the Holy Spirit operates. He places dreams within our hearts in the form of godly desires. *"Delight thyself also in the LORD; And he shall give thee the desires of thine heart" (Ps. 37:4 see also Ps. 21:2).* I'm now living in much of the fulfilment my previous dreams, but now I dream even bigger dreams for the future. God has a big heart, so His dreams for us are much better than we could ever anticipate. You get to adopt His own perspective of who you are. His outlook is way better than yours. This is how the Holy Spirit enlightens our hearts.

Dreams & the Power to Overcome

There is another important reason why it is so important to live with a vision from God. All of us will face struggles and failures that could potentially cause us to give up. The Father shows us what we need to know concerning the future, to provide strength to overcome the challenges we all must face. Usually, a prophetic word reveals the fulfilment of God's promises to us, but it rarely reveals the process it takes to get there. This process will involve struggles, pain, and a lot of challenges. This does not sound very encouraging, but the process fulfills an important role.

The Father has designed our process of walking out the vision to purify our motives and bring us to full maturity, so that we can steward the blessing that God wants to give. This will happen through the pressure and hardships we will inevitably face on our journey to see the promises fulfilled. The pain and struggle of the process will force us to mature so that we can steward the blessings that God gives. That will conform us into the image of Christ and advance the Kingdom of God through us. In the Old Testament we find the story of a man whose life in many ways is a perfect illustration of this. We will now take a brief look at the life of Joseph to gain some insight into the process of seeing God-given dreams being fulfilled.

Joseph - Tested by the Word of the Lord

We find the story of Joseph in Genesis chapter 37-50, but one of the psalms gives us a summary of his life that shows us how the process of going from vision to fulfilment looks like and what it accomplishes in our lives. *"Moreover He called for a famine in the land; He destroyed all the provision of bread. He sent a man before them—Joseph—who was sold as a slave. They hurt his feet with fetters, He was laid in irons. Until the time that his word came to pass, the word of the Lord tested him"* (Ps. 105:16-19 NKJV). The phrase to remember from this passage is *"the Word of the Lord tested him"*.

I want to give a brief overview on how Joseph was tested by the word of the Lord. Joseph was betrayed by his brothers and sold as a slave to Egypt (Gen. 37:1-36). There he ended up serving in Potiphar's house. *"The Lord was with Joseph, and he was a successful man; and he was in the house of his master the Egyptian"* (Gen. 39:2 NKJV). Joseph had favor with Potiphar, and he became a steward over all of Potiphar's house. Because Joseph refused to sleep with Potiphar's wife, even though she continually tried to seduce him, she falsely accused him of trying to rape her. As a result, Joseph was thrown into prison (Gen 39:7-20).

In the prison, the fact that God was with Joseph gave Him favor with people in places of authority. It is an extraordinary situation when a man in charge of a prison trusts a prisoner to steward the prison. This was exactly what happened to Joseph. Joseph met two other prisoners there. Both these men had worked very close to Pharaoh. One of them was Pharaoh's chief butler and the other one was his chief baker. Both had also received prophetic dreams that they didn't understand. Joseph received the interpretation to their dreams from the Lord. According to the interpretation the baker should be killed in three days, while the butler should be released and return to his work. Things developed exactly like Joseph had foretold based on their dreams. But once Joseph's prophetic interpretation was proven to be true, the butler forgot about Joseph.

Joseph himself had received prophetic dreams from God, but for these dreams to come to pass, Joseph had to be through a process of becoming ready to steward the promises of God. This process involved being betrayed by his brothers and thrown into a pit. He was then sold as a slave and he was being falsely accused, which led to his imprisonment. Finally, Joseph was brought into the palace, which turned out to be the place where the promises finally was fulfilled. That miracle happened when Joseph was brought in before Pharaoh to interpret his dreams.

Joseph's Dreams Came to Pass

Joseph asked God for wisdom to interpret Pharaoh's dreams. He received the interpretation, which provided a heavenly strategy that revealed how they could survive the coming famine. It was as a warning concerning this famine that God had given in these dreams to Pharaoh. This in turn led to Joseph's full restoration and Him seeing the promises of God being fulfilled. *"The king sent and released him, The ruler of the people let him go free. He made him lord of his house, and ruler of all his possessions, To bind his princes at his pleasure, And teach his elders wisdom"* (Ps. 105:19-22 NKJV). Here we see an important consequence of Joseph's dreams being fulfilled. It led to the people of God being brought into a place of provision and safety. There they were blessed with great increase and spiritual strength. *"Israel also came into Egypt, and Jacob dwelt in the land of Ham. He increased His people greatly, and made them stronger than their enemies"* (Ps. 105:23 NKJV). Later when Joseph looks back at the sufferings and struggles that he went through, he tells his brothers: *"But as for you, you meant evil against me; but God meant it for good, in order to bring it about as it is this day, to save many people alive"* (Gen. 50:20 NKJV).

Here Comes the Dreamer!

I wanted to share the story of Joseph as an encouragement to all of us. Joseph's brothers called him the dreamer, but it was not a compliment. They called him that because they were jealous and wanted to ridicule him. They hated his dreams to the point that they were prepared to kill him to stop them from being fulfilled. *"Here comes the dreamer!" they said. "Come on, let's kill him and throw him into one of these cisterns. We can tell our father, 'A wild animal has eaten him.' Then we'll see what becomes of his dreams"* (Gen. 37:19-20 NLT). Some people will ridicule you as well, for the same reason that they ridiculed Joseph. They become jealous and angry because of the favor of God upon your life. Remember that Satan is a dream killer and he will use people to try to steal your dreams. When someone calls me a dreamer and tell me that I am too heavenly minded to be any earthly good, I always take that as a compliment. The truth is that it is when we are dreamers and heavenly minded that we are any earthly good!

Your Dreams and Visions Will Be Fulfilled

Our dreams and visions will come to pass. However, if we don't understand the process it will take to birth a vision, we might be tempted give up and become discouraged. Joseph was tested by the word that God had spoken to Him, and we will be tested as well. These tests will purify our motives and cleanse our hearts, so that we can serve people from a pure heart. This is the reason that it sometimes takes longer than expected for God's promises to come to pass. He is preparing us for the blessing He is about to release upon our lives. These blessings will always bring new life and revelation to the body of Christ. They are never given for the sole purpose of strengthening us as individuals. God wants our breakthroughs to advance His purposes for the body of Christ. That alone makes it worth walking through the process, even if we must wait and be patient. If you are being tested by the Word of the Lord right now, don't be discouraged. Keep on praying and dreaming big because what God has showed you will come to pass!

Walking According to the Vision

As Paul is recounting his life-changing encounter with Jesus on the road to Damascus while testifying before king Agrippa, he shares how Jesus spoke to him about his calling. This gave Paul a renewed vision of the future. After Paul had spoken about his encounter, he made this comment: *"Whereupon, O king Agrippa, I was not disobedient unto the heavenly vision" (Acts 26:19).* We need to learn from Paul's example. He did not just sit around waiting for the promises of God to be fulfilled. He aligned his life with what God had spoken. We need to learn from this principle. As the Holy Spirit imparts vision, we can walk according to it by making the changes necessary to see God's Word fulfilled. These changes don't always need to be big, but often we will be led to take many small steps in the right direction. That will take us a long way. If you know that you are called to preach, set some time apart every day to study the Bible, read books and listen to podcasts. That will help you to get the word into your heart, and whatever you have in your heart will sooner or later come out.

How to Be a Visionary Dreamer

There are simple steps that you can take to steward the dreams and visions that God has placed in your heart. I want to share a few the steps I have taken to align myself with God's dreams and visions for my life:

1. **Write It Down.**
    When God has given you a vision, it is important that you remember it and make it concrete. One of the best ways to do that is to write down the vision. I keep all the important prophetic words that I have received in a file on my phone, so that I can read them and meditate on them as often as I need to. I have discovered that this has been a great way to help me keeping the vision alive in my heart, and it is a great source of encouragement to read and be reminded of the promises of God.

2. **Meditate and Pray over the Vision.**
    Meditating and praying over what God has given to you is a key to gain more insight and to internalize what He has spoken to you. God wants his word to become so one with you that it becomes part of who you are. His vision for you will then become your lifestyle.

3. **Create an Action Plan.**
    It is important to create a simple action plan concerning how to begin fulfilling the vision. When I receive a vision from God, I always create a plan that consists of smaller and attainable goals that I can reach easily. Being able to

reach the smaller goals will create a momentum and give confidence to know that you will fulfill the bigger vision one day. We fulfill our visions one step at a time. Having an action plan will helps to define the next step.

4. **Share the Vision with the Right People.**
   One of Joseph's biggest mistakes was that he spoke to his brothers about his dreams. That caused him heartache and a lot of pain. This will happen to us as well, if we share what God has spoken with the wrong people. We need to have wisdom when it comes to which people, we can share our dreams with. I have learned to only share my heart with the people that I know will encourage and support me. That gives me the strength and motivation to believe and pray for my dreams to be fulfilled.

5. **Take Small Steps to Align Yourself with the Vision.**
   When we know what God has planned for us, we should start to align our lives with what He has revealed. Long before I started to write books and preach, I had made it a habit to fill my heart with the Word of God. Over time, the Word of God that I had put into my heart started to overflow. Being able to write this book and travelling all over the world to preach is a result of that. If you have a vision to be in inner healing ministry, you could start by take some counseling classes. If you are called to work with media, find someone who can train you in that area.

6. **Keep on Dreaming and Praying Big.**
   No matter how much we see and experience with God, we always must keep on dreaming. The most important ingredient when it comes to be a Kingdom dreamer is to dream and pray for big things. God always has more for you and me!

CHAPTER 15: FINDING MENTORS & WISE GUIDANCE

In this chapter and the next, we will be studying the importance of mentors and receiving wise guidance. In the next chapter, we are going to look at how to discern the wisdom of Jesus, but here I want to share some thoughts about the need for mentors and wise instruction. Paul reveals what the wisdom of God is in the beginning of his first letter to the Corinthians:

For the Jews require a sign, and the Greeks seek after wisdom: but we preach Christ crucified, unto the Jews a stumbling block, and unto the Greeks foolishness; but unto them which are called, both Jews and Greeks, Christ the power of God, and the wisdom of God. Because the foolishness of God is wiser than men; and the weakness of God is stronger than men (1 Cor. 1:22-25).

Jesus Himself is the wisdom and power of God. This means that receiving wisdom from another person is to hear Jesus speak to us through him or her. The words of Jesus Christ impart spiritual substance and life to us. That makes true wisdom very valuable, and one way to receive it is by discerning when Jesus speaks to us through other people. We are going to take some time to study how we can do that. As we are looking into this topic, we need to keep in mind that true wisdom is found by hearing the voice of Jesus, either directly or through another believer. In a way, this is a subjective experience. Learning to discern His voice through other people takes time, but we have some helpful guidelines in the Bible that point us in the right direction. We will look at them soon, but first I want to mention something about the importance of being influenced by people who walk in the wisdom of God.

The Importance of Wise Guidance

The book of Proverbs highlights the importance of receiving wise guidance. Choosing not to listen to mentors or have any input at all will set us up for failure. *"Where no counsel is, the people fall: But in the multitude of counsellors there is safety"* (Prov. 11:4). But the opposite is also true. When we surround ourselves with mentors and wise people, we gain free access to their good strategies and wisdom to overcome in the spiritual battles. *"Plans are established by counsel; By wise counsel wage war."* (Prov. 20:18 NKJV). We are presently living in a time where we are exposed to more voices and impressions than ever. This has made it more important than ever to discern who we should allow to speak into our lives.

The passages above show us that fulfill to God's calling, we need many wise counselors and good mentors. There will always be a lot of spiritual warfare against us when we're walking with God. To win the war, we need wise guidance. *"Surely you need guidance to wage war, and victory is won through many advisers"* (Prov. 24:6). In my experience, choosing whom we allow to shape our lives is the key to a fruitful life with God. It is important enough to be considered as a spiritual discipline. My own life has been shaped by the influence of a few very good mentors and counselors. The input they have given has been more important than I could ever describe with words. They have spoken the wisdom of Jesus and revealed His heart to me in some amazing ways.

Reasons Why Mentors Are Needed

We need to establish why we need mentors in the body of Christ. Some people wonder if mentors are important, and some totally reject the idea mentorship, since they believe that being guided by the Holy Spirit is enough. But since one of the most common ways the Holy Spirit speaks to us is through other believers that assumption is a big mistake. We need good guidance and advice from other people to do what we are called to do. Here are some important things that good mentors provide:

- **Mentors Encourage and Support**
  A good mentor is someone who has gone before us. The mentor know how tough life with God can be, since they have already faced many of the challenges that we will come across. Their experience has given them wisdom to encourage and support us in what we are called to do.

- **Mentors Inspire and Give Permission to Succeed**
  A mentor inspires, both by sharing their experiences and their testimonies. They have gone further in areas where we long to grow and can show us how to grow in these areas in order to succeed. They give us a good possibility to succeed through their example. They are forerunners who shows us that it is possible to break out of boxes and take new ground for the Kingdom of God

- **Mentors Provide Wisdom and Insight**
  A mentor possesses insights and wisdom that they have gained through walking with God, sometimes at a very high personal cost. By listening to their advice and input, we can get these insights and wisdom at a low price or even for free. We need that since it will save us a lot of time and help us avoid traps that could otherwise have caused us a lot of frustration and pain.

- **Mentors Challenge and Correct**
  When we find a mentor, we find someone who has more experience and therefore has a much longer perspective on life. A mentor can challenge and correct our views on certain issues. We all need to be challenged to see things and to do things differently. Mentors will help with that.

- **Mentors Instruct**
  Sometimes we're lacking the wisdom we need to apply our knowledge. A mentor will help us to take our vision from dream to reality. They help us to put our plans into action by instructing us how to do it.

Different Mentors for Different Areas of Life

We need different mentors who can help us in different areas of life. A mentor is a person that has gone before us. They are our personal forerunners. They have already reached where we want to go. You can have one mentor that helps you in your ministry, another who speaks into your relationships and marriage, and a third when it comes to our health and good eating habits. Always choose a mentor who is more advanced in the area where you need to grow. A mentor should be someone who you respect and trust. We might not always be able to have a personal connection to the people we consider as our mentors, but a great way to be mentored is to study the recorded or the written material of that person. The Bible shows us several different levels of mentoring. Not all these levels involve personal interaction with the mentor.

Biblical Examples of Mentors

We can find many very inspiring illustrations of good mentoring by looking at biblical examples. Even though the word mentor is not used in the Bible, we find many powerful examples of good mentoring happening. The ultimate example is Jesus mentoring the disciples. It is always fascinating to study the life of Jesus, and I have enjoyed studying the way Jesus trained His disciples. It has helped me to understand His dealings with me. By looking at how Jesus ministered to people, we find a biblical pattern for different levels of mentoring. These levels of mentoring were as follows:

- *The multitudes (Matt. 5-7, 15:10-14, 23:1-36).*
  Jesus mentored the crowds and multitudes by preaching and teaching, but also through his healing ministry. That would be equal to mentor people through our seminars, books and recorded material.

- *The seventy (Luke 10:1-24).*
  Jesus trained seventy disciples, that he sent out to preach the gospel and minister to the people. That can be equal to mentor people through discipleship schools and by different forms of ministry training.

- *The twelve apostles (Matt. 10:1-14, Luke 6:12-16).*
  After spending a night in prayer with His Father, Jesus picked the twelve apostles that he trained personally. He shared life with them and spent personal time answering questions and instructing them.

- *The three (Matt. 17:1-13, Mark 5:35-42, 13:3-37).*
  Within that group of twelve Jesus chose three disciples, Peter, James and John, who became his inner circle. They were granted even more access to Jesus, being with Him at the mount of transfiguration and being asked to watch and pray with Him in the garden of Gethsemane.

We can learn a lot from the example of Jesus, both when it comes to receiving mentorship through these different levels. But also, by building our own ministries after Jesus' pattern. By following his example, we can mentor people on many different levels and in many ways. Other very good biblical examples of mentorship would include:

- Barnabas & Paul (Acts 9:26-28, 11:20-26).
- Paul & Timothy (Acts 16:1-4, Phil. 2:19-24, 1 Tim. 1:2).

- Moses & Joshua (Exod. 17:8-16, 24:12-14, 33:9-11, Numb. 13-14, 27:15-23.)
- Samuel & David (1 Sam. 16:1-13).
- Elijah & Elisha (1 Kings 19:15-21, 2 Kings 2:1-18).
- Jehoiada the priest & King Joash (2 Kings 11:1-12:16, 2 Chron. 22:10-24:16).

Christlikeness & Mentorship

It is important to remember that mentorship in the Kingdom of God is always built on Christlikeness. A mentor doesn't need to be in an official leadership position. Just because someone carries the official title of pastor, priest or theologian doesn't guarantee that this person a good mentor. A mentor in the Kingdom of God, need to be someone who knows the heart of the Father and walks in intimacy with Jesus. It would therefore be a big mistake to look for mentors only on the official christian platforms. Always look for people who lives a powerful life with the Father in the secret place. A mentor needs to know the heart of the Father, walk in Christlikeness and in the power of the Holy Spirit.

The Effects of Good Mentorship

A mentor always leads us to where they have gone themselves. For example, when Elijah was taken up to heaven in a chariot of fire, Elisha was ready to step into the role of a prophet to the nation of Israel. But there is one example that has become my personal favorite, and that is that of Benaiah. He serves as a good example of how good mentorship help us in our transformation into "beast killers" and "giant slayers". Benaiah was one of king David's mighty men. These mighty men were king David's own heroes, who supported him in the establishment of his reign and kingship. They were his most outstanding warriors and fighters. One of them was Benaiah and we can read about him here: *"Then*

Benaiah the son of Jehoiada, the son of a valiant man of Kabzeel, who had done great deeds, killed the two sons of Ariel of Moab. He also went down and killed a lion in the middle of a pit on a snowy day" (2 Sam. 23:20). He was a valiant warrior who killed both giants and a lion. Benaiah had been raised up and mentored by king David, who is known to be a giant slayer and who had killed wild beasts to protect his sheep several times (1 Sam. 17:20-58).

We always reproduce in others what we have in our hearts. The name Benaiah is interesting because it means *"built up by God"*. He was built up to become a hero who could overcome in battles and face wild beasts in a pit. This is a picture of our lives as well. The Father is building us up, but He will not do it independently of other people. One of the ways in which He uses people in the process of building us up, is through our mentors. They build us up by sharing their experiences, which helps us to grow in our identity and calling.

The Tragedy of Rejecting God's Gift of Mentors

King David had probably taught these principles to his son, king Solomon. Solomon was a wise man who wrote a lot on the need for godly counsel and mentors. In fact, we have already quoted some of his statements on this topic in this chapter. However, Solomon's son, Rehoboam, seemed to have missed his teaching in this area, because he suffered the consequences of rejecting the mentors God had appointed for him. When Rehoboam inherited the throne and became king after his father had passed away, the people of Israel made the following request to king Rehoboam, concerning his leadership style: *"Your father made our yoke heavy; now therefore, lighten the burdensome service of your father, and his heavy yoke which he put on us, and we will serve you"* (1 Kings 12:4). The people promised to serve king Rehoboam, if he would only lighten the burden of work that his father had put on them.

As a new and inexperienced king, he made a wise decision when responding: *"Depart for three days, then come back to me." And the people departed. Then King Rehoboam consulted the elders who stood before his father Solomon while he still lived, and he said, "How do you advise me to answer these people"* (1 Kings 12:5-6 NKJV). Rehoboam chose to ask the elders who had walked with his father Solomon during his reign as the king. Before he was backsliding, Solomon was the most prosperous and wise king in the history of Israel. These elders had gained a lot of wisdom by seeing how Solomon ruled as king.

They gave a very good piece of advice to king Rehoboam, but unfortunately, He rejected it: *"If you will be a servant to these people today, and serve them, and answer them, and speak good words to them, then they will be your servants forever." But he rejected the advice which the elders had given him, and consulted the young men who had grown up with him, who stood before him"* (1 Kings 12:7-8). Instead, he asked his friends for advice and they gave a very bad advice (1 Kings 12:10-15). King Rehoboam listened to their advice and contrary to the request of the people, he decided to give a rough answer. As a result, the kingdom of Israel was split in two and king Rehoboam could never reign to the fullest of his potential. He only reigned as king over the tribe of Judah for his seventeen years as king (1 Kings 11:41-12:4, 14:21-31, 2 Chron. 9:29-12:16). By studying this story, we can see what a serious mistake it is to reject the mentors that God has appointed for us. But even more, it should ignite a prayer in us for God to raise up godly mentors in the body of Christ, and for us to have a heart to receive them.

Consequences of Listening to the Wrong Voices

I have received a lot of blessings by being mentored by good people. Unfortunately, I have experienced how painful it can be when I have allowed the wrong people into my life as well. It has caused me some serious heartache and pain at times. But even worse, as illustrated by the example of king Rehoboam, I have also seen how other people's lives have been totally ruined as a tragic result of bad influence and mentorship. Their calling was wasted and they ended up in bondage. *"Do not be deceived: "Evil company corrupts good habits. "Awake to righteousness, and do not sin; for some do not have the knowledge of God. I speak this to your shame" (1 Cor. 15:33-34 NKJV).* The kind of people we keep close to us will be one of the most important factors as to how our lives will turn out. According to my observation, a lot of people have never realized this. As a result, they have never learned how to be intentional with choosing whom they allow to lead them. Paul warns us that bad company will corrupt good habits, potentially even ruin the lifestyle that we have built as a response to the love of God.

We should not be afraid or judgmental of other people and their motives, but we need to be discerning as to whom we permit to speak into our lives. Otherwise, we will end up listening to the voices that speak the loudest and are the most persistent. If we do that, we take a huge risk, since these voices that demand our attention the most, rarely has our best interest in mind. It is much better to be intentional in inviting the right people to influence us. In the next chapter, we are going to look at some insights from the Bible on how to do this.

CHAPTER 16: DISCERNING THE WISDOM OF JESUS

In the previous chapter, we looked at the need for mentors and wise instruction. The challenge that comes with discovering this need is that there are so many voices out there. It is not always easy to find the voices that benefits us the most. For this reason, we need to discern whom we are to allow as an influencer in our lives. Since Jesus is the wisdom of God, we need to listen to His voice through the people and leaders we chose to follow. In this chapter I want to share some insight into how we can do that.

Jesus Speaks Life

The most important characteristic of the wisdom of God is that it always imparts life. When listening to any preacher or counselor, this is how we know that Jesus is speaking to us. *"The Holy Spirit is the one who gives life, that which is of the natural realm is of no help. The words I speak to you are Spirit and life"* (John 6:63 TPT). The words of Jesus are anointed by the Holy Spirit and they have the power to impart grace to the ones listening. When I am listening to a preacher or speaking with a christian friend, I always try to listen with my heart, because life is always imparted to the heart. Knowledge educates the mind, but the life of Christ transforms and quickens our hearts.

I can recognize when Jesus speaks to me through another person by observing what goes on in my heart. Whenever my heart is revived and refreshed by a teaching or advice, I know that Jesus is speaking. Everything that God does in our lives happen within our hearts and when Jesus is speaking, He imparts life and grace to us. When you are being ministered to in a way that revives your spirit and stirs up the life of Christ within you, that is a very good sign that Jesus is using that person in your life. This is often overlooked, but it becomes obvious when we think of how Jesus describes Himself as the life of God: *"Jesus saith unto him, I am the way, the truth, and the life: no man cometh unto the Father, but by me"* (John. 14:6). Jesus is the life of God revealed, and when He came into this world, it was for the purpose *"… that they might have life, and that they might have it more abundantly"* (John 10:10). I have learned not to be overly focused on whether I fully agree with a leader's theology or not, but I want to follow life. Wherever I can taste the life of Christ, I know that I will be blessed and receive wisdom from God.

Life Is to Know the Father

It is important that we understand what type of life we are talking about here. This life is not just about feeling inspired or encouraged, even though that is often the result, when the life of Christ is imparted to us. Jesus defines the meaning of eternal life in the following way: *"And this is eternal life, that they may know You, the only true God, and Jesus Christ whom You have sent"* (John 17:3 NASB). Life is knowing the Father and to know Jesus. Only people who receive Jesus have eternal life, but the manifestation of possessing eternal life is to know the Father and to know Jesus. Therefore, when searching for a mentor, look for the leaders and influencers who know the heart of God. There you will find life, because their influence will impart the love of the Father and the life of Christ!

Three Important Checklists

As we're following the life from Christ, there are three important checklists that I recommend everyone to use as guidelines. These lists reveal the character of Christ, and how His life is revealed through a personality who has been transformed by the love of the Father. These lists are:

1. The Beatitudes
2. The Fruit of the Spirit
3. The Wisdom from above

As we're looking for the type of character we want to find in our mentors and leaders, these lists are unbeatable. I have seen many good descriptions of good character traits within a leader, but no one is better than these, since they describe the character and life of Jesus. He is the best mentor and leader!

1. The Beatitudes (Matt. 5:3-11)

We find the Beatitudes in the beginning of Jesus' sermon on the Mount. They are a good description of what the life and character of Jesus looks like. The whole purpose of this sermon is to reveal the mind and character traits of Christ, so the beatitudes are a description of the attitudes of the one who has been transformed by the life of Christ:

- *Blessed are the poor in spirit, for theirs is the kingdom of heaven.*
- *Blessed are those who mourn, for they will be comforted.*
- *Blessed are the gentle, for they will inherit the earth.*
- *Blessed are those who hunger and thirst for righteousness, for they will be satisfied.*
- *Blessed are the merciful, for they will receive mercy.*
- *Blessed are the pure in heart, for they will see God.*
- *Blessed are the peacemakers, for they will be called sons of God.*

It would be a misunderstanding to believe that Jesus gave us this sermon, expecting us to live by it. That way of thinking only lead to legalism. This sermon is a revelation of Jesus Himself, but also of what His life will look like when being revealed through us. The Beatitudes describe the mind of Christ. Therefore, we should be able to see them in action, at least to some degree in the people that are our leaders and mentors.

2.   The Fruit of the Spirit (Gal. 5:22-23)

The fruit of the Spirit reveals the character of God and when we receive from the life of Christ, it will always be flavored by the fruit of the Spirit. The Bible speaks of the fruit of the Spirit as one fruit. This is because all the other fruits grow from the love of the Father. When we have been rooted in the Father's heart, the fruit of the Spirit will grow in our lives. Paul describes the fruit of the Spirit in Galatians:

- *Love*
- *Joy*
- *Peace*
- *Patience*
- *Kindness*
- *Goodness*
- *Faithfulness*
- *Gentleness*
- *Self-control*

We cannot produce these fruits by ourselves. They grow as we abide in the Father's love. As the life of Christ is formed within us, our lives will reveal these fruits. Spiritual ministry imparts the life of Christ to us. When that life is imparted by a mentor or leader it will be flavored by the fruit of the Spirit.

3.   The Wisdom from Above (Jam. 3:17-18)

James wrote many important things on the wisdom of God in his letter. As He writes on the wisdom of God, he is revealing the life and character of Christ, since Jesus is the Wisdom of God. This is how James describes divine wisdom: *"But the wisdom from above is first pure, then peace-loving, gentle, reasonable, full of mercy and good fruits, impartial, free of hypocrisy. And the fruit of righteousness is sown in peace by those who make peace"* (Jam. 3:17-18 NASB). As we abide in the love of the Father, our lives will be shaped by the wisdom of God, which will reveal the life of Jesus Christ through us. The life of Jesus looks like the *"wisdom from above"*, and when we are looking for mentors and wise leadership, we need to look for the life of Christ being expressed through them. Everyone longs to have mentors who walk in the wisdom from above. This is the character of the wisdom from above:

- *Purity*
- *Peace-loving*
- *Gentle and Reasonable*
- *Loving Mercy*
- *Being Impartial*
- *Free of Hypocrisy*

Jesus is the wisdom of God, but He is also the power of God that transforms our character so that our lives can reveal the wisdom from above. Look for these character traits when you chose who to mentor or leader.

Attitude, Fruit & Character

We have seen that wherever the life of Jesus is revealed, we can see the attitudes found in the Beatitudes, and taste the fruit of the Spirit. We will meet the wisdom from above there. We should be able to find all of these to a high degree in the people that mentor and leads us. Of course, no one walks in these character traits in a perfect way. Only Jesus can measure up to that standard, but it is important that we can find some of these attitudes and fruits within our leaders and mentors.

The Fruit of Demonic Wisdom

Right before writing on the wisdom from above, James describes the fruit of demonic wisdom. It is worth reading what he wrote about the demonic wisdom here, as a contrast to the wisdom that comes from God. *"But if you have bitter envy and self-seeking in your hearts, do not boast and lie against the truth. This wisdom does not descend from above, but is earthly, sensual, demonic. For where envy and self-seeking exist, confusion and every evil thing are there"* (Jam. 3:14-16 NKJV). Demonic wisdom is built on selfishness. When a person is trapped in the web of demonic wisdom, their life will be filled with selfish ambition and envy toward people. This type of wisdom always manifests in confusion and relationships filled with strife. We should be careful with people if we perceive that they are driven by selfish ambitions.

Since selfish ambitions manifests as envy and striving, I have learned to be cautious with people who are critical and look for the worst in other people. Criticism usually comes from a root of selfish ambition. We have seen that wherever the life of Jesus is flowing, that we can *feel* His life and *see* the character of wisdom in action, but we can also *taste* the fruits of the Spirit among mentors and leaders that lives by the life of Christ.

Wisdom Comes as We Practice the Word of God

"Therefore whosoever heareth these sayings of mine, and doeth them, I will liken him unto a wise man, which built his house upon a rock: and the rain descended, and the floods came, and the winds blew, and beat upon that house; and it fell not: for it was founded upon a rock" (Matt. 7:24-25). When we know that as Jesus is speaking, His words will impart spiritual life, we can draw the conclusion that revelation is never mere knowledge. Revelation from God will always lead to a transformed lifestyle, which means that a wise leader walks by the light and revelation they have received from God.

When we're receiving insight through revelation, we're gaining true understanding. Understanding is transformed into wisdom as we practice what we know. We should not trust a teacher or leader who does not practice what they preach. We get practical wisdom by living out the revelation that we have received. Life is full of trials and as Peter writes:

These trials will show that your faith is genuine. It is being tested as fire tests and purifies gold—though your faith is far more precious than mere gold. So when your faith remains strong through many trials, it will bring you much praise and glory and honor on the day when Jesus Christ is revealed to the whole world (1 Pet. 1:7 NLT).

Genuine faith is always proven by the trials of life. As we stand firm and overcome, we build a stable character. This is the way to grow into a trustworthy person. Such a man or woman have gained a wisdom that is built on both knowledge and experience. It is important that we make sure that the people speak into our lives and mentors us practice what they preach.

For example, if someone wants to give me advice about healing ministry, I want to know if that person heals the sick. Likewise, if someone wants to counsel me about marriage or family, I want to know if their own marriage is healthy. It is dangerous to allow people to teach us based on knowledge alone. It is not enough to have a theological education or biblical knowledge to become a good leader. That can even become a hindrance if that education becomes a source of authority for us. We need people who walk with the Father and whose life is filled with the fruit of intimacy with Him. A good mentor needs to be in the constant process of being conformed into the image of Christ. Remember that we are to follow life. A life lived in fellowship with Jesus will result in wise counsel and leadership.

Wisdom & the Power of God

We read earlier that Jesus Christ is both *"the power of God, and the wisdom of God" (1 Cor. 1:24)*. It is impossible to separate the power of God from His wisdom. Consequently, a wise person flows in the power and anointing of the Holy Spirit. Paul said that *"your faith should not stand in the wisdom of men, but in the power of God" (1 Cor. 2:5)*. Our faith should be based on the power of God, not on human arguments. By knowing the wisdom of God, we will also know His power. It is a sign of wisdom to desire the gifts of the Spirit and to move in the power of God (1 Cor. 14:1). I always look for people who walk in the power of God when I'm looking for good teaching and advice. In my experience, they usually go together.

People can at times be too impressed by leaders who operates in the power of the Holy Spirit, only to be disappointed when these leaders fall into sin. Sometimes, it has then been stated that our character is more important than walking in the gifts of the Spirit. I understand where that way of thinking comes from, but I can't fully agree. Walking in the power of God is part of a Christlike character. Granted, it is not the only part of wise leadership, but it is still an important part. Wise leaders and mentors are usually men and women who walk in the power of God.

Wisdom Can Be Revealed from Unexpected Sources

Although the wisdom of the Father is usually revealed through the body of Christ, sometimes His wisdom can be revealed from unexpected sources as well. As an example of this, we find that Paul quoted some Greek philosophers, both in his letters and in his sermons (see Acts 17:28, Tit. 1:12). Jesus can also speak to us through our culture. For example, He can speak though secular songs or movies. Sometimes, the wisdom of God is even revealed through the people that we would deem as enemies of the truth.

King Josiah met a tragic end, all because of his failure to perceive the voice of God through king Neco, who God wanted to use to speak to him (2 Kings 23:28-30, 2 Chron. 35:20-27). You probably remember king Josiah from an earlier chapter, where we studied his life and the revival that he brought to the nation of Judah. But the same king who had such a humble heart before God and His Word, now failed to discern the voice of God through king Neco. Because of this, he attacked the Egyptian army, who had been sent by God toward the Assyrian army and king Josiah died in that battle. This shows how important it is to discern the wisdom of God. We need be humble enough to receive His wisdom, even if He chooses to speak to us through an unexpected source. But as already stated, the most common place to find the wisdom of God is through the body of Christ.

The Wisdom of the World vs. the Wisdom of God

Paul makes it clear that the wisdom of God and the wisdom of the world are of different kinds. He writes: "*...Christ sent me not to baptize, but to preach the gospel: not with wisdom of words, lest the cross of Christ should be made of none effect. For the preaching of the cross is to them that perish foolishness; but unto us which are saved it is the power of God*" (*1 Cor. 1:17-18*). We can learn worldly wisdom through studies and life experience. It is possible to gain biblical knowledge in a worldly way. We can do that by studying certain subjects in the Bible without knowing Jesus. This is the reason that theology can sometimes become powerless and quench our spiritual life.

God's wisdom is of a different kind and it is only available by knowing Jesus. He is the wisdom of God and by growing in our relationship with Him, we gain access to the wisdom of God. It is for this reason *"... that God hath chosen the foolish things of the world to confound the wise; and God hath chosen the weak things of the world to confound the things which are mighty"* (1 Cor. 1:27). God's plan is to use the people who is foolish and weak in the eyes of the world to reveal the wisdom of God. He is doing this, so that in the end, everyone will see the foolishness of trying to be wise without knowing Jesus. He is the manifestation of the Father's wisdom. Knowing Jesus is true wisdom. It is important that the people that influences us knows Him well enough to discern the difference between the wisdom of God and the wisdom of the world.

How to Find Mentors & Wise Guidance

A lot of people are longing to find good mentors. This is a very good desire but finding them is not always easy. I'm blessed with very good mentors and their input is very valuable to me. Here are some of the things to look for when you need wise counsel:

1. **Follow Life**

   As we have seen in this chapter, when Jesus speaks to us through a teaching or advice, it always revives our spirit and impart His life. Go where you find life and freedom of Christ. Religious input might sound very good, wise and balanced, but it always creates a spiritual heaviness and oppression. When I'm getting and input that impart new life to me, it has always led me in the right direction. Always follow life!

2. **Remember the Character of Wisdom**

   In this chapter, we have studied what the character of a wise person looks like. Remember the three checklists that we studied- the Beatitudes, the fruit of the Spirit and the Wisdom from above. Go back and read them again from time to time. These are the character traits that we are looking for in our mentors and leaders. We have also seen how a wise person has been growing in wisdom by practicing their understanding of the Word of God, and that a wise person walks in the power of the Holy Spirit. It is a good idea to be aware of this when you are looking for a mentor.

3. **Choose Mentors for Different Areas of Life**
    Many people are looking for one person to mentor them, but that is a bad idea. No one is equipped to speak into every area of your life. I have at least three mentors that I speak with regularly. They help me with different areas of my life. I have also been mentored by the books and podcasts produced by people that have come further in the areas where I want to grow. There is both strength and safety in a multitude of advisers. You know who is equipped to help you in a certain area by the fruit they bear in that area.

4. **There are Different Levels to Mentoring**
    You can be mentored on different levels. Remember that all mentoring doesn't need to happen through a personal connection. I 've been mentored by some people through reading their books and receiving from their teachings. I've been mentored by others by watching their example. Finally, I have mentors that sit down with me every now and then to address different areas of my life. I call them personal mentors. I would advise you to intentionally be mentored in all these levels as well.

5. **Ask Someone Who Knows**
    If I want to know something about an area of ministry or life, I rarely sit and wait for God to send someone to me. I ask someone who is advanced in that specific area. As I started to write my books, I realized that I needed help,

so I asked for advice from some authors that I knew, who had written the type of books that I wanted to write. I received some good input from them. I try to do that in every area where I need to grow with Christ, and I have discovered that there are many kind people in the body of Christ who loves to help us when we ask.

6. **Personal Mentorship Grows Organically**
    There are exceptions, but to be assigned with a personal mentor rarely works very well. This type of relationship requires a high level of trust and vulnerability. Because of this, we shouldn't be too quick to choose a mentor. It takes time to develop trust. When you surround yourself with good people and ask questions, these relationships will grow naturally into mentoring relationships. In that way, the mentorship you need will emerge naturally.

7. **Find People that Can Strengthen you in your Gifts and Calling**
    A good mentor should always hold you accountable to reach your full potential in Christ. Accountability is not meant to just prevent you from moral failure, but to help you be and do everything that you are called to be and do. This should be your goal when you influence other people as well. We should always aim for helping people to reach their full potential in Christ!

CHAPTER 17: DESIRE SPIRITUAL GIFTS

"Follow the way of love and eagerly desire gifts of the Spirit, especially prophecy" (1 Cor. 14:1 NIV). Paul encourages us to live in the love of God and to flow in the gifts of the Spirit. To follow the way of love means abiding in the love of the Father, but also to let Him bring healing and restoration to the world through us. A tangible fruit of abiding in His love is that we will constantly be growing in love for people, which means having a growing desire to bring them into an encounter with the heart of God. This is where the spiritual gifts come in. They are God's equipment so that we can love people His way.

The gifts of the Holy Spirit are the love languages of Heaven and as soon as we start to grow in love, our desire for these gifts will grow as well. Love is more than an attitude or affectionate feeling toward another. The Father's love is an active power that deeply transforms the person who wants to receive it. I have discovered that whenever I get to see new depths of the Father's love, my desire and passion to flow in the anointing always increases. The love of God is a fire that burns for the freedom and restoration of every human being. For this reason, partnering with the love of the Father will lead us into lifestyle filled with manifestations of the gifts of the Spirit. Desiring spiritual gifts is an issue of loving people because we need the power of God to minister to a world in pain.

Manifestations of the Holy Spirit

The gifts of the Spirit are supernatural manifestations of the Holy Spirit, meaning that they are the ways in which the Holy Spirit choses to manifest Himself through a specific person, at a certain occasion. The Holy Spirit distributes these gifts as He wills. *"But the manifestation of the Spirit is given to each one for the profit of all" (1 Cor 12:7) NKJV).* In 1 Corinthians 12 Paul teaches that the gifts of the Spirit are expressions of the Spirit Himself. The Holy Spirit reveals His love and power to us and bestows us with the power we need to minister to certain needs. These gifts do not belong to the person operating in them, but to the Holy Spirit. The gifts of the Spirit are not natural talents or motivational gifts. All of us possess natural gifts as part of who we were created to be. Some people are very practically gifted, while others are good when it comes to administration. These are natural gifts, while the gifts of the Spirit are manifestations of the Holy Spirit Himself. This means that operating in spiritual gifts it not something that we learn by practicing spiritual formulas. We are always dependent on the Holy Spirit, so to operate effectively in these gifts, we need to know the Giver of the gifts.

The Gifts of the Spirit

For to one is given by the Spirit the word of wisdom; to another the word of knowledge by the same Spirit; to another faith by the same Spirit; to another the gifts of healing by the same Spirit; to another the working of miracles; to another prophecy; to another discerning of spirits; to another divers kinds of tongues; to another the interpretation of tongues: but all these worketh that one and the selfsame Spirit, dividing to every man severally as he will (1Cor.12:8-11).

We clearly see here that God wants all believers to operate in the gifts of the Spirit. The reason for that is to reach the world with the gospel and to build up of the body of Christ. We have already seen that the gifts of the Spirit are the love languages of heaven because they are the way in which the love of God is expressed to the world. To better understand these gifts, a simple definition of each of the nine gifts mentioned in 1 Corinthians 12 is needed. Since I wrote about the gifts of the Spirit in my book, *Transformed by the Grace of God,* I will only give brief description of these gifts here. The gifts of the Holy Spirit are usually divided into three categories, based on how they operate. These categories are:

- **The revelation gifts.** These are the gifts that *reveal* something.

The word of knowledge is a supernatural revelation given by the Holy Spirit about past or present circumstances. This gift releases knowledge about locations, people, or even events that we could know nothing about in the natural. This gift is a great help when we minister to people in bondage that come to us for healing. The Holy Spirit gives this gift, so that we can get to the real root much easier. Then we can minister healing and freedom effectively.

The word of wisdom is a supernatural revelation from the Holy Spirit concerning the plans and strategies of God concerning the future. This gift is a great help, both when it comes to missionary work, challenging situations and when we are planning the next step of our visions.

Discerning of spirits brings supernatural revelation of the realm of the spirit. We then perceive, see, or hear what is really going on in the spiritual realm, both with the angels and demons. This gift has nothing to with faultfinding or criticism. It gives us the ability to discern the spiritual influences behind the scenes.

- **The power gifts.** These are the gifts that *do* something.

The gift of faith is a special faith that the Holy Spirit gives as a supernatural manifestation to us. This is an impartation of God's own faith, so that we can receive a miracle or a breakthrough that is above our own level of faith. Sometimes we face situations that are so challenging that our own faith is not enough and then God shares His faith with us so that we can receive the miracle or breakthrough we need.

Working of miracles are acts of power where the Holy Spirit supernaturally intervenes to override the natural laws to give us a miracle. Sometimes we need unusual miracles that is more than just a simple manifestation of the power of God. This gift imparts the boldness and strength for us to release such a miracle.

The gifts of healing are manifestations of the power of the Holy Spirit to bring supernatural healing to the soul and body of those who are sick or broken. This is the only gift that is mentioned in plural because it can manifest in many ways. This gift is closely associated to the healing anointing and it usually releases a lot of healing miracles all at once.

- **The utterance gifts.** These are the gifts that *say* something.

The gift of prophecy is a supernatural message coming forth in a human language, given by the Holy Spirit through the believer. Moving in this gift means that we speak forth the messages that Jesus gives to us. This could be done as a direct message, through visions or through prophetic preaching and teaching.

The gift of speaking in tongues is now available to every believer through the baptism of the Holy Spirit (Mark 16:17). Every child of God can function in the devotional aspect of this gift. Speaking in tongues is our personal prayer language, through which we're speaking mysteries to God and building up our inner man (1 Cor. 14:2, Jude 20). In a public setting, people can deliver a prophetic message in tongues. This message needs to be interpreted.

The gift of interpretation of tongues is a supernatural gift given by the Spirit to interpret your own prayer in tongues, or a public message given in tongues. This is often the gift that opens the door to the prophetic realm. We should all pray for the gift of interpreting tongues (1 Cor. 14:13-15). This gift will reveal the mysteries of God that was given in tongues.

As He Wills

"But one and the same Spirit works all these things, distributing to each one individually as He wills" (1 Cor. 12:11 NKJV). Since the gifts of the Spirit are manifestations of the Holy Spirit, we cannot control them or decide when we want to operate in them, but we can and should desire them. We can grow in our intimacy with the Holy Spirit, so that our heart becomes aligned with His. In this way, we can stay available to Him all the time. We do that by abiding in the love of the Father. Abiding in His love makes our hearts soft and moldable in His hands. This will help us to cultivate a lifestyle of yielding to the Holy Spirit. The Holy Spirit distributes His gifts when and to whomever He wants but the Holy Spirit is usually more eager to minister to people than we are. As we stay aligned with the heart of the Father, we will flow in these gifts more often than we might expect since Jesus is always ready to love people though us.

God Loves People More Than We Do

Knowing that the Father loves people much more than I do has made it much easier for me to flow in the gifts of the Spirit. Before I understood this, I was very analytical and self-conscious in this area because I believed that the Holy Spirit only wanted to work through me if I was prepared enough. That is not the case at all. He is much more eager to release His power than we are to flow with it. He will take every chance He get to reveal who Jesus is by signs, wonders and miracles.

One time God spoke to me about this in a conference. As I was resting in my room preparing to preach, I was very tired and felt more ready to go to bed than to preach and pray for people. As I was praying in my room, the Holy Spirit showed me that God loves people much more than I do. He longed to heal and deliver the people attending the conference. The only thing I needed to do was to preach Jesus and the power of the cross. The Holy Spirit would do the rest. That is what happened. A lot of people experienced powerful deliverances from demonic bondages and deep healing at this conference. Jesus is more than eager to love people through you and me!

This might sound self-evident, but there is a difference between knowledge and revelation. Knowledge provides information, but revelation provides spiritual sight. As the Holy Spirit spoke to me, I suddenly saw the heart of the Father toward His people. By seeing His love and compassion for broken hearts, I realized that I could relax and just show up to share the gospel, trusting the Holy Spirit to do the rest. This revelation has stayed with me through the years and it has proven to be true time and time again. God does not need our perfect preparation. He just needs our willing hearts and the Holy Spirit does the rest!

Edifying the Body of Christ

One of the main reasons for the gifts of the Holy Spirit is the edifying and building up of the Father's family. *"And the same is true for you. Since you are so eager to have the special abilities the Spirit gives, seek those that will strengthen the whole church"* (1 Cor. 14:12 NLT). As we have seen, we cannot love the Father and not love His children as well. Abiding in the love of the Father transforms our heart so that what is important to Him becomes important to us as well (John 5:19). The plan of the Father is to raise up a big family of sons and daughters that reflects who Jesus is. Jesus is focused on the same goal, which is building His church and He identifies with us so much that we have been made one spirit with Him (1 Cor. 6:17). When we are in alignment with His heart, our desire will be to see the church restored and built up. Since the Holy Spirit is always working toward this goal, we are then positioned to operate in spiritual gifts.

The Greater Gifts

There is an important principle about flowing in the gifts of the Spirit that reveals how we can release the love of the Father more effectively through these gifts. That is that we are to desire the greater gifts. Paul calls some of the spiritual gifts greater, but it is not because some are better than others. Neither is he implying that a person who prophesies is better than the one who speak in tongues. The greatest gifts are the ones who reveal the love of the Father the most in a certain situation.

Some of the spiritual gifts are greater in a gathering of believers because they edify more in that setting. *"I wish you could all speak in tongues, but even more I wish you could all prophesy. For prophecy is greater than speaking in tongues, unless someone interprets what you are saying so that the whole church will be strengthened"* (1 Cor. 14:5 NLT). The gift of Prophecy is more important than tongues when believers gather. The reason is that prophecy encourages, comforts, and edifies the body of Christ (1 Cor. 14:3). Paul spoke in tongues a lot, but in a gathering of believers he wanted to say something that would help the people present in the meeting. *"I thank God that I speak in tongues more than any of you. But in a church meeting I would rather speak five understandable words to help others than ten thousand words in an unknown language"* (1 Cor. 14:18-19 NLT). Prophecy is very important when it comes to the building up of the believer, so it becomes a greater gift in that context. In a different context, other gifts might be greater and more needed. For example, when Jesus gives the great commission, calling us to reach the world with the gospel, other manifestations of the Spirit are highlighted.

Spiritual Gifts and Evangelism

Jesus has sent us into all the world to preach the gospel (Mark 16:15-16). As Jesus sent us, He promised that supernatural signs and wonders would follow: *And these signs shall follow them that believe; In my name shall they cast out devils; they shall speak with new tongues; they shall take up serpents; and if they drink any deadly thing, it shall not hurt them; they shall lay hands on the sick, and they shall recover"* (Mark 16:17-18). Jesus promises that the Holy Spirit will confirm the preaching of the gospel with healings and miracles of deliverance. When it comes to reaching the lost, these gifts are needed and therefore become greater in that context. Signs and wonders always draws people to Christ. They become signs that point to Jesus and become powerful demonstrations of the love of God. Our Father wants to bring all his lost children back home again and the gifts of the Spirit becomes powerful manifestations of His heart as they are used to bring in the harvest. A big part of responding to His love is to desire the spiritual gifts that reveals His love the most in every situation. When we operate in the gifts of the Spirit, people will encounter the heart of the Father.

Depending on the Supernatural Work of the Holy Spirit

As we read through the book of Acts and the gospels, both Jesus and the early church were fully dependent on the power of the Holy Spirit. When Luke describes the ministry of Jesus Christ, he writes: *"And Jesus returned in the power of the Spirit into Galilee: and there went out a fame of him through all the region round about"* (Luke 4:14). Peter describes the ministry of Jesus in a very similar way, while preaching in the house of Cornelius: *"... how God anointed Jesus of Nazareth with the Holy Ghost and with power: who went about doing good, and healing all that were oppressed of the devil; for God was with him"* (Acts 10:38). To live in Christlikeness means walking in the power and anointing of the Holy Spirit, proclaiming freedom to the captives and bring deliverance to the oppressed.

When studying the ministry of Jesus, as well as the ministry of the early church, we find that miracles opened whole regions to the gospel and that their mission trips were orchestrated through the leading of the Holy Spirit. If we want to reveal the love of the Father and the beauty of Christ to the world, we need the gifts of the Spirit more than ever. In many of the nations to which I travel to preach, it is impossible to do any work that bears fruit, unless we are moving in the power of the Holy Spirit. These cultures are steeped in a belief in the supernatural and it is common in these places that the witchdoctors and priests of other religions moves in demonic signs and wonders. This is becoming more common in the western world as well. I am convinced that all missionary work and evangelism that is not followed by signs and wonders, will become increasingly irrelevant. If we're abiding in the love of the Father and long for other people to be transformed by that same love, the gifts of the Spirit and the power of God is not optional. We need a new, fresh anointing so that we can reveal His love to a broken world.

Flowing in the Gifts of the Spirit

As we have seen earlier, we do not own the gifts of the Spirit and we can't learn to operate in them, just by using certain techniques or principles. We are always dependent on the Holy Spirit, but there are still keys that can help us in yielding to the Holy Spirit, and to stay available to Him:

1. **Cultivate Intimacy with the Holy Spirit**
    The most important thing as we desire spiritual gifts is to know the Giver of the gifts. For example, when we learn to discern His voice, it will be much easier to move in the prophetic. We get to know His voice and His heart by spending time with Him. Throughout this book, we have already talked about several things that we can do to cultivate a deeper relationship with the Holy Spirit. Prayer, worship, soaking, fasting and reading the Bible are great ways to spend time with Him. To practice these habits regularly helps us to grow in intimacy with God.

2. **Realize that God Loves People More than We Do.**
   God is much more interested in people encountering His heart than we are. We never need to convince the Spirit to bestow spiritual gifts to us. It is the other way around. He always wants to reach people with His love, and He is looking for someone who is available to flow in the power of the Holy Spirit. This realization has helped me a lot. He is not looking for me to be perfect, but He wants me to be available.

3. **Ask for the Gifts You Desire the Most**
   When the Holy Spirit wants to use you more often in a certain gift, it usually starts with Him putting a desire to operate in that gift within your heart. My experience is that when I have responded to that desire by praying for these gifts to manifest, they have started to operate more frequently through my life. This is a way to co-labor with God. He puts a desire in your heart and you respond by praying for it. As a result, that gift start to flow through you.

4. **Step out in Faith**
   You need to expose yourself to situations where the gifts of the Spirit are needed if you want to operate in them. The Holy Spirit will not give you gifts if there is no need for them. If you desire to see the sick healed, you need to start praying for the sick. Some of the greatest miracles I have ever witnessed has been when I have put myself in situations where great miracles where needed. There are many ways you can step out in faith. The Holy Spirit is longing for you to make yourself available to Him in this way, so that He can release the love of God through you.

CHAPTER 18: A GENEROUS LIFESTYLE

Our Father is very generous. He loves us with an everlasting love and He always wants to give us the best that He has to offer. Love motivated our Father to give the most precious and costly gift that has ever been given. He gave His only Son. *"For God so loved the world, that he gave his only begotten Son, that whosoever believeth in him should not perish, but have everlasting life" (John 3:16).* By giving Jesus for us, our Father has demonstrated His generosity to us. The Father revealed how valuable we are to Him. Nothing was more precious to the Father than His only Son, Jesus Christ, and since He gave Him for us, we can conclude that He will hold nothing back. Paul asks a question along this line: *"He that spared not his own Son, but delivered him up for us all, how shall he not with him also freely give us all things" (Rom. 8:32)?* This is a rhetorical question. The answer is obvious to anyone who knows the Father even a little. It was His pleasure to bless us with all the riches of heaven. *"So don't ever be afraid, dearest friends! Your loving Father joyously gives you his kingdom with all its promises" (Luke 12:32 The Passion)!* We have been blessed with all spiritual blessings, and these blessings are our inheritance as His children. He is a very generous God and because that is who He is, generosity is one of the core values of the Kingdom of God.

Generous Giving is a Lifestyle

Even though we will address money in this chapter, generous giving relates to much more than just our finances. Generosity is a lifestyle that reflects the heart of the Father. Sharing life with others means being generous with everything that we possess, including things like our time, attention, forgiveness and prayer. It means being filled with and to flow in the self-giving love of

Jesus Christ. In my previous book, *Abiding in the Father's Love*, we studied how the glorious freedom of the children of God could be summed up in one simple word: Christlikeness. One of the most powerful ways to reflect the life of Jesus is to be a cheerful giver. After all, His mission was to give His life to redeem us and bring us back home to the Father. When we're developing a habit of generosity, we continue in His mission by reflecting the heart of God, so that the Holy Spirit can use our lives to bring the lost back home to the Father.

Becoming a Cheerful Giver

"But this I say: He who sows sparingly will also reap sparingly, and he who sows bountifully will also reap bountifully. So let each one give as he purposes in his heart, not grudgingly or of necessity; for God loves a cheerful giver" (2 Cor. 9:6-7 NKJV). As we are giving cheerfully, we are reflecting the heart of the Father because He is the most cheerful giver of all. He gives to everyone who asks willingly and without criticism (Jam. 1:5) Doing what we see the Father doing not only includes being led by the voice of the Holy Spirit, but it also means becoming so one with His heart that our lives reveal His character. Therefore, we are not becoming givers by learning the principles of giving, but by knowing His heart. The Bible has a lot to say about the principles of giving, but generosity grows in our heart as we learn to receive and abide in the love of the Father. As we are transformed by His love, we will find more joy in giving because it will become our nature to be generous. Jesus gave His life to provide financial restoration and blessing. *"For you know the grace of our Lord Jesus Christ, that though he was rich, yet for your sake he became poor, so that you through his poverty might become rich"* (2 Cor. 8:9 NIV). Jesus broke the curse of poverty and blessed with financial prosperity through the cross. This is our birthright as children of God.

Our Father Wants us to have an Abundance to Give

And God is able to make all grace abound toward you, that you, always having all sufficiency in all things, may have an abundance for every good work (2 Cor. 9:8).

When we embrace a lifestyle of giving and generosity, our hearts are aligned with His. He will then make sure that we are blessed with abundance, so that we can give more. Our Father wants to have children who has more than enough, so that they can bless every good work and demonstrate the generosity of heaven. Few things have spoken so powerfully to me about the love of God, as when I have been generously blessed by one of His children. I can recall several times when someone has given me a gift from God, and it never gets old. It has been even more amazing when I have been able to bless other people with gifts.

When generosity and giving becomes our lifestyle, the love of the Father will be revealed among us and we will see a supernatural transfer of wealth. The book of Acts connects this type of lifestyle with the move of the Holy Spirit and revival in the early church. I believe this applies to our days as well. A generous person is someone who has created a lot of room for the Holy Spirit within his or her life!

Sharing What We Have

As believers we are called to be one in mind and heart, living out the unity we have in Christ. This was modeled in a powerful way by the church in Jerusalem. *"All the believers were one in mind and heart. Selfishness was not a part of their community, for they shared everything they had with one another. The apostles gave powerful testimonies about the resurrection of the Lord Jesus, and great measures of grace rested upon them all (Acts 4:32-33 TPT).* Living like this requires that we develop a generous lifestyle, where we learn to share life together. This is not limited to only our money, but it includes our time and attention, gifts and possessions, as well as our home.

This radical generosity was connected to the great measure of grace that rested upon the early church. Grace is God's ability that empowers us to be and do everything that we are called to be and do. When we cultivate a unity of heart that is based on a lifestyle of sharing with one another great grace will be released. This will help to meet the needs in our churches, in part because of generous gifts, but I believe that such a lifestyle attracts a supernatural grace for wealth and abundance. This is what happened in the church in Jerusalem as this grace manifested: *"Some who owned houses or land sold them and brought the proceeds before the apostles to distribute to those without. Not a single person among them was needy"* (Acts 4:34-35 TPT). The depths of the love of God will be revealed in a community that embraces radical generosity in this way.

Grace for Radical Generosity

This means that there is a grace for generosity and giving. This grace equips us to give way more than what is possible in natural circumstances. Our goal needs to be to walk in this supernatural grace all the time. We see this powerfully demonstrated when Moses collected an offering for the building of the tabernacle. *"And they came, every one whose heart stirred him up, and every one whom his spirit made willing, and they brought the LORD's offering to the work of the tabernacle of the congregation, and for all his service, and for the holy garments"* (Exod. 35:21 see also Exod. 35:26, 29). Notice that their heart was stirred up so that their spirit became willing. It was the grace and anointing for radical giving that stirred them up so that they wanted to give in this generous way. The people gave an extravagant gift that day. In fact, they gave so much that Moses had to tell them to stop giving:

The people bring much more than enough for the service of the work which the Lord commanded us to do." So Moses gave a commandment, and they caused it to be proclaimed throughout the camp, saying, "Let neither man nor woman do any more work for the offering of the sanctuary (Exod. 36:5-6 NKJV).

Reading about how the Israelites gave such an extravagant gift always challenges me deeply. It inspires me to ask the Father to release this anointing upon His people again! We need this grace of generosity to fuel our giving so that we can finance all the expenses of extending the Kingdom and preaching the gospel all over the world. Imagine when we flow in such generosity that the leaders of our churches must tell us to stop giving because we have been given to much. That will lead to the great transfer of wealth that God has promised His people!

Grace That Attracts Wealth and Abundance

We find a powerful promise about the transfer of wealth in the book of Isaiah: *"Then you will see and be radiant, And your heart will thrill and rejoice; Because the abundance of the sea will be turned to you, The wealth of the nations will come to you"* (Isa. 60:5 NASB). This promise is given in the middle of a prophecy concerning the glorious church that will rise as we embrace our identity as His favored people. There is a big transfer of wealth that will happen when we get deeper revelations of the Father's goodness. The Father wants to give us more than enough, and for us to have so much favor upon us that Jesus shines forth through our lives, all over the world. Isaiah begins the prophetic statement that I just quoted by declaring:

Arise, shine; for your light has come, And the glory of the Lord has risen upon you. For behold, darkness will cover the earth And deep darkness the peoples; But the Lord will rise upon you And His glory will appear upon you. Nations will come to your light, And kings to the brightness of your rising (Isa. 60:1-3).

As we flow in the grace of generosity and abundance we will rise and shine so that nations and kings will be drawn to us to receive wisdom and revelation. They will see the beauty of Jesus Christ through us!

Becoming Safe for Abundance

Sometimes the objection that money is the root of all evil is being raised when I preach on financial blessing and abundance. That is not what the Bible says in the passage that is referred to by the people who raises this objection. This is what Paul wrote:

Those who want to get rich fall into temptation and a trap and into many foolish and harmful desires that plunge people into ruin and destruction. For the love of money is a root of all kinds of evil. Some people, eager for money, have wandered from the faith and pierced themselves with many griefs (1 Tim. 6:9-10 NIV).

It says that the love of money is *a* root of all kinds of evil, not that it is *the* root of evil. Even though this objection is usually rooted in religious thinking there is some truth in it. This is a warning to people who want to get rich and whose motivation is the love of money. I don't think this would apply to most of us though, because our motivation is to love the Father and reflect His heart. As His love fills our lives, we want to have an abundance because we want to be cheerful givers. Abiding in His love will make us safe for financial blessings because our motivation will be love for the people in need.

The solution to being snared by the love of money is not to be poor. Rather, the way to break the power of greed is by growing in generosity. Jesus said that *"No man can serve two masters: for either he will hate the one, and love the other; or else he will hold to the one, and despise the other. Ye cannot serve God and mammon"* (Matt. 6:24). We need to remember this warning when we are studying generosity and abundance. However, as Jesus continues to teach, He encourages us to trust our Father to provide for us as we seek the Kingdom of God: *"But seek ye first the kingdom of God, and his righteousness; and all these things shall be added unto you (Matt. 6:33).* Our focus should always be to build a deeper relationship with the Father and to live generous lives, but at the same time we can trust our Father who lavishes His love and abundance upon us so that we can give even more to every good work!

Sowing and Reaping

Even though giving starts with our hearts being transformed by the love of the Father, there are still biblical principles of giving. One such principle is sowing and reaping.

Be not deceived; God is not mocked: for whatsoever a man soweth, that shall he also reap. For he that soweth to his flesh shall of the flesh reap corruption; but he that soweth to the Spirit shall of the Spirit reap life everlasting (Gal. 6:7-8).

The world operates by the principle of working and earning, but the Kingdom of God operates by sowing and reaping. Whichever seed we sow, we will always receive back in the form of a greater harvest. If we want to see good fruit in our relationships we need sow love, kindness, and grace into those relationships. The same is true when it comes to our financial situation. It is good to work hard and to have a good work ethic, but the main key to financial breakthrough is our giving. We could never outgive God and the measures by which He gives back will always be greater than the ones that we use to sow.

Generosity and our Attitudes

The principle of sowing and reaping applies to much more than our finances. It applies to all areas of our lives. If, for example, we want to develop good and healthy relationships this principle is very important. In fact, Jesus addressed our attitudes toward other people when He taught on sowing and reaping:

Do not judge, and you will not be judged. Do not condemn, and you will not be condemned. Forgive, and you will be forgiven. Give, and it will be given to you. A good measure, pressed down, shaken together and running over, will be poured into your lap. For with the measure you use, it will be measured to you. (Luke 6:37-38 NIV).

One of the characteristics of a generous man or woman is being able to forgive quickly, and to be slow to judge and condemn. It is the nature of generosity to give people the benefit of the doubt, by always seeing the best in them. I have learned this by being an itinerant preacher, who minister in different churches. Many of these churches may hold to doctrines that I might not agree with, their expressions of worship might differ from mine and they sometimes hold to traditions that I do not adhere to.

When I began as an itinerant preacher years ago, I was quick to major on the differences in belief and practice in the churches I visited, just to find what separated us. In my heart, I held some judgement against people who in my estimation held to wrong thinking and adhered to dead traditions. That resulted in me being much more limited in the way I could serve them. Through the years I have come to realize that Jesus is way more generous and patient than I was back then. As I have been growing in love, I have started to see the body of Christ, more through His eyes and today my focus has shifted so that I no longer notices these differences in the same way. My focus has shifted to what Jesus is doing in the churches where I minister. It is so much more fun to have a generous attitude towards people. This change of focus has released a new level of favor in our ministry. Of course, not everybody likes me, but most churches and leaders are extremely generous to me. We need to take every chance we can find to sow mercy, grace and kindness. After all, we need lots of it ourselves!

Waiting for the Harvest

One of the reasons why we lose our harvest is that are we are expecting quick results. When we are not seeing the fruit as fast as we expected, we grow impatient and give up. Paul encourages us to *"…not be weary in well doing: for in due season we shall reap, if we faint not. As we have therefore opportunity, let us do good unto all men, especially unto them who are of the household of faith" (Gal. 6:9-10).* It takes time for the harvest to grow, so we need to learn the art of waiting patiently. While we are waiting for the harvest, we are to keep on sowing generously, knowing that our Father will make good on His promise. Paul encourages us to do good toward all men, but especially to our fellow believers.

As we keep on doing that we will reap in due season. We do not always know when that season comes, but it will come because that is the way the Kingdom of God operates: *"The Kingdom of God is like a farmer who scatters seed on the ground. Night and day, while he's asleep or awake, the seed sprouts and grows, but he does not understand how it happens" (Mark 4:26-27 NLT).* We do not know how the seeds grow into a harvest, but we can trust God to make it happen.

Just as we have laws of nature, there are laws of the Kingdom of God. One such law is that seed always produces a greater harvest after its own kind. This is how the Kingdom of God operates, and this law is meant to operate on our behalf in a very organic way. When we learn to cooperate with this law, we can be intentional in what kind of seeds we sow and how much, knowing that the harvest will come sooner or later. *"The earth produces the crops on its own. First a leaf blade pushes through, then the heads of wheat are formed, and finally the grain ripens. And as soon as the grain is ready, the farmer comes and harvests it with a sickle, for the harvest time has come"* (Mark 4:28-29 NLT).

Developing a Generous Lifestyle

Generous giving reveals the self-giving love of Jesus. As we are being transformed into His image, generosity will increasingly become one of our noticeable character traits. All areas of life will be affected as we develop a habit of generous giving. In the list below, I will be mentioning some areas where our generosity can become a blessing to other people:

1. **Time and attention**
   A lot of people are very lonely today. In fact, loneliness could be spoken of in terms of a pandemic in our society. The biggest reason for that is that we are living in a very individualistic culture. Inviting people into our lives by giving time and attention is a big deal in a society like ours. We need to be intentional in doing this because our society has conditioned us to walk through the day with our attention focused on our own needs. We can break that cultural conditioning by intentionally making room for other people in our daily life. By being generous with our time and attention, we demonstrate the love of God.

2. **Mercy and Forgiveness**
   We saw earlier that a generous person possesses a heart that is slow to judge and condemn, but quick to forgive. People will always need mercy and forgiveness, but the experience of many has been that there are very little to be found. Since we know the Father, we have an eternal fountain of mercy and forgiveness to drink from, which

means that we can share it generously with other people. The healing power of the mercy and forgiveness of God is amazing and life changing. Let's share it as generously and as often as possible!

3. **Encouragement**

Another characteristic of generosity is that it always sees the good in other people. A generous person loves to lift and encourage. I have seen the power of encouragement in my own life many times. When I have walked through tough seasons, God has sent the right people into my life to encourage and strengthen me. Their kind words have been such a help and motivator for me. Our Father is the ultimate encourager. We have the privilege of reflecting His heart by being encouragers who stands with people in their challenges!

4. **Money**

We have already looked at the area of generosity and money, but this is well worth mentioning again. Blessing people with financial gifts is great joy, because it is part of our new nature. Ask the Holy Spirit if He wants to use you to bless someone with a financial gift today, or if He wants you to donate to a certain church or ministry!

5. **Our Talents and Gifts**

Another valuable thing to share is our God-given talents and gifts. One of the reasons we are gifted so differently is that God doesn't want us to fulfill our calling without our brothers and sister in Christ. We need their gifts and input to fulfill God's calling. Since God's way of working with us is through relationship and friendship, fulfilling His will always include other people. We are called to be generous in helping other people to develop in their God given purpose. We have gifts that they don't possess and by helping them succeed, we will advance the Kingdom of God and fulfill our own destiny.

6. **Our Testimony and Experience of Living with God**
Our testimony and experiences with God are valuable. You can help a lot of people by sharing your experiences of walking with God. The people that are listening to you can receive freely from the insights that you have gained by paying a very high price. You can invest a lot in other people by sharing what you have learned during your walk with God.

7. **Our Prayer and Intercession**
We can be generous with our time and attention by taking time to pray for people every day. I have made it a habit of praying for people as soon as the Holy Spirit put them on my heart, or even when I hear that someone have a challenge or a spiritual attack to deal with. Prayer and intercession are ways through which we can partner with God. We can be generous by taking time to pray for people.

8. **Our Hospitality**
Having an open home where people are welcome can be a great gift. I remember what an impact it had on me just to see healthy Christian families and homes. Realizing that it is possible to build a heathy, Christ-centered home brought a lot of comfort and healing to my heart. I got healed by the power of Christ through the hospitality of brother and sisters in Christ. I am not alone in having an experience like that. Welcoming someone as a guest in your home can bring a lot of hope and healing to that person. Since salvation is to come home to the Father's house, hospitality is a powerful way to reflect His loving heart to the world.

CHAPTER 19: REACHING THE WORLD WITH HIS LOVE

All power is given unto me in heaven and in earth. Go ye therefore, and teach all nations, baptizing them in the name of the Father, and of the Son, and of the Holy Ghost: teaching them to observe all things whatsoever I have commanded you: and, lo, I am with you always, even unto the end of the world. Amen (Matt. 28:18-20 NKJV).

It is hard to mention the love of the Father without thinking of missions as well. One of the most famous verses in all the Bible speaks about God's love for the world, resulting in a missionary movement. *"For God so loved the world, that he gave his only begotten Son, that whosoever believeth in him should not perish, but have everlasting life. For God sent not his Son into the world to condemn the world; but that the world through him might be saved"* (John 3:16-17). The Father loves the world and He does not want anyone to perish. That was the Father's motivation for sending Jesus into the world and His heart is filled with a passionate longing for every human being to come back home to Him. *"For this is good and acceptable in the sight of God our Savior, who desires all men to be saved and to come to the knowledge of the truth"* (1 Tim. 2:3-4). It is impossible to abide in the love of the Father and not growing in a desire to reach people with the gospel. It is because of the desire within the heart of God for the world to come back home to Him, that Jesus sent us to make disciples of all nations.

The Father's Desire is our Mission

By finding ways to get involved in missions we are responding to the deepest desire in the Father's heart, since He has always wanted a big family. When Jesus told us to go into all the world to preach the gospel, it is an invitation to cooperate with Him, so that He can get what He desires the most. This is an invitation to share in His compassion and love with the world. The heartbeat of all true missionary work must have as its focus to reach people with the good news of Jesus Christ and the cross. It is only by knowing Jesus that people can come to the Father. Every other activity in the Kingdom of God, needs to be a fruit of us knowing the heart of the Father through Christ.

As we read how Jesus sends us into all creation, we can hear the longing in the heart of the Father for humanity to return home. *"Go into all the world and preach the gospel to all creation. Whoever believes and is baptized will be saved, but whoever does not believe will be condemned"* (Mark 16:15-16 NIV). Responding to this call means that we align with what the Father is longing for, which means that we are partnering with His love to reach the world with the gospel.

Expecting Signs and Wonders to Follow

Jesus promises that as we preach the gospel, we can count on the Holy Spirit to provide supernatural assistance by confirming our proclamation of the gospel with miracles:

And these signs will accompany those who believe: In my name they will drive out demons; they will speak in new tongues; they will pick up snakes with their hands; and when they drink deadly poison, it will not hurt them at all; they will place their hands on sick people, and they will get well (Mark 16:17-18 NIV).

The Holy Spirit always glorifies Jesus and one of the ways that He does that is through signs and wonders. The gifts of the Spirit are the love language of heaven and few things testifies about the love of the Father as powerfully as miracles. All true evangelism is meant to be power evangelism. The love of Christ is an active power that brings healing and deliverance wherever it manifests.

Flowing in the gifts of the spirit is not an issue of us preferring to be charismatics or not; it's an issue of love. Our loving Father will do whatever is necessary to bring people home to Him and since signs and wonders testifies so powerfully about Jesus, we should desire them deeply.

Power Evangelism Has Impacted Me in a Big Way

I have personally witnessed many instances when miracles of healing and deliverance led to the salvation of many. It has had a strong impact on me to have had the honor to preach the gospel in nations where I'm unfamiliar with the culture and I can't even speak their native language. In these nations, I have seen Jesus open blind eyes and deaf ears, while we were praying for people. I have watched how Jesus delivers from demonic bondages and baptizes hundreds of people in Holy Spirit and fire (Luke 3:16). Signs and wonders are powerful demonstrations of the love of the Father. and it reveals His heart like nothing else. I have gotten to know His heart and seen His love in deep and profound ways, as I have flowed in the gifts of the Spirit. Signs and wonders have then been released to draw lost souls home to the Father through Jesus Christ.

The Love of the Father is an Active Power

The love of the Father is an active power that saves and delivers from the power of darkness. The power of His love flow through ordinary people like you and me. I have decided to go on mission trips every year to share the love of Christ with the world in this way. He promised us that we could *"Ask of Me, and I will give You the nations for Your inheritance, and the ends of the earth for Your possession" (Ps. 2:8 NKJV).* The Father spoke these words to Jesus Christ, but we are His representatives in the earth today, so this promise applies to us as well. We have been made heirs of the world through the blessing of Abraham. This means that we can come to the Father and ask for the nations (Rom. 4:13). As we respond to the love of God by saying yes to preaching the gospel, we become part of the Father's plan to reach people groups and nations. We will participate as they're transformed by the love of God. Jesus has opened the way back home to the Father for every human being through the cross. Jesus has carried away the sin of the world and reconciled us with the Father. Nothing can hinder an open heart from receiving salvation through Jesus Christ.

Jesus has Taken Away the Sins of the World

When John testified about Jesus, he proclaimed boldly: *"Behold the Lamb of God, which taketh away the sin of the world" (John 1:29).* Jesus succeeded in His mission. The sins of the whole world have already been taken away. The world has now been reconciled back to God through Jesus Christ. The Father is waiting for His lost children to come home: *"For God was pleased to have all his fullness dwell in him, and through him to reconcile to himself all things, whether things on earth or things in heaven, by making peace through his blood, shed on the cross" (Col. 1:19-20 see also 1 John 2:1-2).* Through Jesus Christ, all things on earth and in heaven have now been reconciled to the Father. Jesus has carried away the sins of the world and opened a new and living way back to the Father. Sin will never again be a hindrance for people who want to come to God. We have the wonderful privilege to proclaim this good news to the world. Through Jesus, the door has now been opened to come home to the Father, through the new and living way that Jesus has opened through the cross.

Be Reconciled to God!

Paul writes in his second letter to the Corinthians: *"Now all things are of God, who has reconciled us to Himself through Jesus Christ, and has given us the ministry of reconciliation, that is, that God was in Christ reconciling the world to Himself, not imputing their trespasses to them, and has committed to us the word of reconciliation" (2 Cor. 5:18-19 NKJV)*. Again, we can clearly see that God doesn't impute sins and trespasses to the world, because Jesus has already dealt with the issue of sin on the cross. As Paul continues, he explains how we have been given the ministry of reconciliation. We have now received delegated authority from Jesus Christ to proclaim this good news, all over the world: *"Now then, we are ambassadors for Christ, as though God were pleading through us: we implore you on Christ's behalf, be reconciled to God. For He made Him who knew no sin to be sin for us, that we might become the righteousness of God in Him" (2 Cor. 5:20-21 NKJV)*. People are reconciled back to God as they believe the gospel in their hearts and respond by confessing Jesus as Lord (Rom. 10:9-10).

Reconciled by His Death - Saved by His Life

The world has been reconciled to the Father by the finished work of Jesus, but it is through responding to the gospel by confessing Him as Lord that a person gets saved. *"Much more then, being now justified by his blood, we shall be saved from wrath through him. For if, when we were enemies, we were reconciled to God by the death of his Son, much more, being reconciled, we shall be saved by his life" (Rom. 5:9-10 NKJV)*. Some people have concluded that since Jesus has reconciled the whole world to God, every human being will be saved in the end. The thought process of this teaching is that God wants everyone to get saved and He is powerful enough to make it happen. Another assumption is that God in His sovereignty will trump the free will of man, so that even people who haven't received Jesus, will still be saved in the end. That is not true. This teaching undermines both the seriousness of sin and the freedom of man.

The forgiveness of sins is necessary, but not enough. People who have been dead in sin need to be made alive again. Humans need an impartation of the life of Christ to get saved and born again.

Only Jesus can impart the life that raises us from spiritual death. *"And this is the record, that God hath given to us eternal life, and this life is in his Son. He that hath the Son hath life; and he that hath not the Son of God hath not life" (1 John 5:11-12).*By receiving Jesus as Lord and Savior, man receive eternal life. Man does not possess eternal life without receiving the life of God. *"He that believeth on the Son hath everlasting life: and he that believeth not the Son shall not see life; but the wrath of God abideth on him" (John 3:36).* Jesus is the tree of life, and by receiving Him, people gain access to eat from the fruit of that tree. The life of God will be imparted and the person who receives that life is born again. In the new birth, we have received God's everlasting life and we have full freedom from all guilt and condemnation (John 5:24).

Motivated by the Love of Christ

We have seen that when we are being rooted in the love of Christ, His desires and passions will become ours. It is easy to see what the motivation of Jesus is. *"For the Son of Man has come to seek and to save that which was lost" (Luke 19:10 NASB).* When Jesus spoke of that which was lost, He meant the Fathers lost children that has yet to return home. Jesus Christ is motivated by a passionate and burning love for the lost. He wants to receive a huge reward for His suffering. His reward is the lost souls that return home to the Father through receiving Jesus as their Lord and Savior. The apostle Paul reveals the heart of what motivates Jesus within this passage: *"It is a trustworthy statement, deserving full acceptance, that Christ Jesus came into the world to save sinners, among whom I am foremost" (1 Tim. 1:15 NASB).* Jesus came into this world to bring the lost souls back to the Father. The more we come to know the heart of Christ, we will become increasingly more motivated by this as well. The deeper our relationship with the Father becomes and the more we walk in intimacy with Jesus, the more we will be longing to reach the world with the gospel. Paul wrote that he was compelled by the love of Christ to preach the gospel all over the world (2 Cor. 5:14-15). This is the main difference between a religious approach to evangelism, compared to an approach that grow from knowing the heart of God. A religious approach tells us that we should evangelize to be good Christians and show our gratitude to Christ. Doing it as a response to the love of the Father gives us permission to do it because we now see people through His eyes. In religion we *must* witness, but in the Kingdom of God, we *get* to preach the gospel.

Being Burned by Religious Pressure to Evangelize

I understand that some of you might have been badly burned by a legalistic approach to evangelism. I have met many good and honest believers who have felt driven by guilt to evangelize. This has pushed them into doing things they didn't want to do. If that applies to you, I'm not writing to tell you that you should ignore the pain and neither do I mean to push you into "just getting over it and try harder". I'm writing to invite you to an encounter with the healing love of Christ. Give your disappointments and pain to Him, so that He can comfort and restore your heart. Let Him wipe your mind clean from all religious sermons you have heard on missions and evangelism. Let Him fill you with the love of the Father for the people who are still lost in sin and darkness. There is deep healing in encountering His love in a deeper way.

The Heart of Jesus

Then Jesus went about all the cities and villages, teaching in their synagogues, preaching the gospel of the kingdom, and healing every sickness and every disease among the people. But when He saw the multitudes, He was moved with compassion for them, because they were weary and scattered, like sheep having no shepherd (Matt. 9:35-36 NKJV).

In this text, we find several important keys to keep in mind when we are studying evangelism. Whenever Jesus was preaching and teaching, miracles of healing followed Him. Jesus wants this to be our normal way of preaching as well, since the gospel releases the power of God. Signs and wonders follow the proclamation of Jesus Christ.

Another important thing to notice, is that while Jesus watches the people and see them in all their pain and brokenness, His heart is moved with compassion. We need to walk in the compassion of Jesus while we minister. What motivated Him to preach the gospel must to be our motivation as well. Jesus' response to the pain and needs that He observed among the people Was to call us into fervent prayer: *"The harvest truly is plentiful, but the laborers are few. Therefore, pray the Lord of the harvest to send out laborers into His harvest"* (Matt. 9:37-38 NKJV). We should make it a main part of our prayer life to ask the Father to send workers to the harvest. Our problem is not that the harvest is not ready. People are more open for the gospel than ever before, but they are waiting for us to share it with them. Our problem is that we need more laborers because the harvest is so big.

The Harvest is Ready

One of the greatest deceptions of the devil is in trying to convince us that people are not interested in hearing the gospel. He wants to deceive us into believing that we should stay silent, since no one wants to listen to us preaching the gospel of Jesus any way. That is a big fat lie! The fields are ripe for harvest right now.

You know the saying, 'Four months between planting and harvest.' But I say, wake up and look around. The fields are already ripe for harvest. The harvesters are paid good wages, and the fruit they harvest is people brought to eternal life. What joy awaits both the planter and the harvester alike" (John 4:35-36 NLT)!

We live in a time when people are increasingly struggling with mental health issues, existential struggles and identity problems. Their hearts are crying out for Jesus Christ, but they don't know who He is yet. There is a greater need than ever for good news that provides hope and healing for the confused and broken soul. We are carriers of the best news in the universe and the harvest fields are ripe and ready for a big harvest right now. As we begin to preach the gospel, the multitudes will encounter Jesus and be brought home to the Father!

We Are in This Together

As Jesus continues His teaching on the harvest of souls at the end of the age, He makes a powerful point: *"You know the saying, 'One plants and another harvests.' And it's true. I sent you to harvest where you didn't plant; others had already done the work, and now you will get to gather the harvest"* (John 4:37-38 NLT). It is our calling to go and make disciples of all nations, but this is not a one man show. This calling was given to the whole body of Christ. The burden to reach the lost never rests on us as individual believers, but on the body of Christ. We are dependent on the grace of God to get the job done and we are laboring together to bring in the harvest.

We may have different roles but we will share the same reward as we present to Jesus the reward of His sacrifice, in the form of lost souls that have been saved! Knowing that we are called to the great commission as the people of God has really helped me to enjoy working with mission. We have different roles and we are going to need all the different expressions, gifts, callings and strengths of the body of Christ to get the job done. But the good news is that this is happening right now. The gospel is breaking through all over the world right now. The vision that the apostle John saw is coming to pass. He saw a great multitude from every nation tribe, language and people group gathered to worship the Lamb of God (Rev. 7:9-10).

The Day That the Holy Spirit Could Not Wait Any Longer

God has always longed for the multitude mentioned in the book of Revelation to come home. There is an event in the book of Acts that reveals just how eager the Holy Spirit was for this to happen. He wanted to break out of the box that He had been placed in because of the misguided belief that the gospel was to the Jews only. The event in question is found in Acts chapter 10 and it is the written account of the first sermon ever preached to gentiles (Acts 10:34-45).

Through the supernatural guidance of the Holy Spirit, Peter had been led to join a group of men who brought him to the house of Cornelius, where a crowd of gentiles eagerly awaited his arrival (Acts 10:1-24). They were all there to hear the gospel. As Peter is preaching, he shares the good news of "... *how God anointed Jesus of Nazareth with the Holy Ghost and with power: who went about doing good, and healing all that were oppressed of the devil; for God was with him*" *(Acts:10:38)*. When Peter comes to the highlight of his gospel presentation, he shares how the forgiveness of sins and a new life is now available through Jesus Christ, something extraordinary happened:

To him give all the prophets witness, that through his name whosoever believeth in him shall receive remission of sins. While Peter yet spake these words, the Holy Ghost fell on all them which heard the word. And they of the circumcision which believed were astonished, as many as came with Peter, because that on the Gentiles also was poured out the gift of the Holy Ghost. For they heard them speak with tongues, and magnify God (Acts 10:43-46).

When forgiveness of sins through Jesus was proclaimed by Peter, the Holy Spirit could not wait any longer. His desire to break out of the religious box He had been put in became too strong, so the

Holy Spirit fell on the gentiles and baptized them in fire right there and then!

The worldview of Peter and the other circumcised believers were shaken as the gentiles were filled with the Holy Spirit and started to speak in tongues. Peter, being the leader of them team, made the only decision possible in that situation: *"Can any man forbid water, that these should not be baptized, which have received the Holy Ghost as well as we? And he commanded them to be baptized in the name of the Lord. Then prayed they him to tarry certain days"* (Acts 10:47-48). This event reveals how eager God was to break out of all man-made limitations to reach people with the gospel. He is just as eager to do that today, which is why we need to tap into divine creativity to join Him in reaching the world with the love of God.

Creativity and Missions

Because the Father loves the world with an everlasting love, He will never give up or take no for an answer. He will always find new ways to reach the nations and He wants us to participate in what He is doing. I am convinced that the Father wishes to give many new creative strategies to reach new people for Jesus when we have a willing heart. This is one of the reasons why dreams, visions and prophetic guidance are a direct consequence of being filled with the Holy Spirit. *"I will pour out of my Spirit upon all flesh: And your sons and your daughters shall prophesy, and your young men shall see visions, and your old men shall dream dreams: And on my servants and on my handmaidens I will pour out in those days of my Spirit; and they shall prophesy"* (Acts 2:17-18). Prophecies, visions and dreams releases the creativity of heaven so that we can reach the world with the gospel in new and fresh ways! The harvest is ripe right now. It is time to reach new people through new ways and strategies that fulfills the great commission. Let's respond to His call and be part of a movement that will reach the whole world with the gospel of Jesus Christ!

New Creative Expressions Will Provoke Criticism

When the church in Jerusalem heard that Peter ministered to and even baptized the gentiles to Jesus Christ, he was brought in by the leaders to be questioned (Acts 11:1-3). This will happen as we pioneer new things in the Kingdom of God. People react in fear and take issue with us. We can learn a lot by observing how Peter handled the criticism he faced. *"But Peter began and explained at length to them in an orderly sequence, saying…" (Acts 11:4 NASB).* Peter did not defend himself or start a debate. He gave a detailed, calm, and logical description of what had happened. He ended his recollection of these events with the following humble words: *"Therefore, if God gave them the same gift as He also gave to us after believing in the Lord Jesus Christ, who was I that I could stand in God's way" (Acts 11:17 NASB)?*

When we are being criticized in our work or ministry, this is a very good example to follow. To calmly share what God has done and explain why we must follow the Holy Spirit, is a good way of keeping our focus on what's important. The devil wants us to get into endless discussions and debates to steal our focus form the heart of the matter, which is to continue walking down the road that our Father has called us to travel together with the Holy Spirit. The people questioning Peter saw the hand of God in this situation and responded very gracefully: *"When they heard this, they quieted down and glorified God, saying, "Well then, God has also granted to the Gentiles the repentance that leads to life" (Acts 11:18).* Our critics might not always respond as nicely as these people did, but we can be determined to handle the criticism that comes against us with the same gentleness and humility as Peter did here. We are called to preach the gospel to all of creation and our time is too precious to waste on religious debates.

Ways to Participate in the Great Commission

We are living in amazing times right now, where it is easier than ever to get involved in mission and evangelism. Today, with all the technology and social media available, there are more ways than ever to participate in reaching the world for Christ. Here are some practical steps we can take to do that:

1. **Being filled with the Compassion of Jesus Christ.**
    We need to ask the Father to fill us with the compassion of Jesus Christ. Compassion needs to be our motivation in all evangelism and mission. As we come to know His heart for the lost, we will gain motivation to win the lost for Christ. We have the privilege of bringing to Jesus that which He has won on the cross. His reward is multitudes from every tribe, people and nation being brought home to the Father.

2. **Short-term mission trips**
    Ever since I got saved, I was gripped with a love and a burden for reaching the nations and I decided early on in my life as a believer to join short term mission trips to different nations. To be able to join a team and travel to another part of the world where we lead people to Jesus Christ, baptize them and watch them get filled with the Holy Spirit is an amazing experience. I recommend that you make it a habit to join mission trips where you can have similar experiences every year. It is a life changing experience!

3. **Online Outreach Ministry**
    The ministry that I'm a part of have started a work online that has led to some very powerful results. Through our podcasts, programs, and social media, we have now seen hundreds of people come to Jesus. Today, we have very

interesting opportunities to reach the nations, which has previously been closed to the gospel and where it is still very hard to travel to preach the gospel. But through the internet, we can now reach them pretty easily. You have an opportunity to reach large parts of the world today, and the only thing you need is a laptop and a creative mind. Let's go online and reach the nations!

4. Prayer & Intercession

We saw how Jesus has called us to pray for laborers to be sent into the harvest field. Taking time to pray and intercede for world missions is one of the important and very good ways to be involved in missions. Intercession, combined with fasting and spiritual warfare, will break open the most closed nations for the gospel. The nations of this world are becoming the Kingdom of our God, and we are called to participate in that through prayer and intercession.

5. Giving

Reaching the world with the gospel costs a lot of money. This is one of the reasons as to why God wants us to be blessed with abundance, so that we can support world missions. In the unlikely case that we are not able to travel to a mission field ourselves, we can still reach that field by giving financial support to them that are going there. And even if we can go to the nations, we should of course take advantage of the wonderful possibility to give cheerfully to missions anyway!

CHAPTER 20: RESTING IN CHRIST

The last spiritual discipline that we're going to study is learning how to rest in Christ. The new covenant is a covenant of rest and we are called to live and operate from a place of rest in Christ. *"Consequently, there remains a Sabbath rest for the people of God. For the one who has entered His rest has himself also rested from his works, as God did from His. Therefore let's make every effort to enter that rest, so that no one will fall by following the same example of disobedience"* (Hebr. 4:9-11 NASB). We should never underestimate the blessing of knowing how to rest. Even God took a day off when He was done working with creation. He finished creating our world by creating Adam, the first human being. Then God rested and that day of rest was the first day in Adam's life. It is significant that his life started with rest.

Before we can do any valuable work in the Kingdom of God, we need to learn how to rest in Christ. In the new covenant, Jesus Himself is our Sabbath rest and through the cross we have been fully delivered from religious striving, so that we can rest from our own works. Resting in Christ is not the same as inactivity. Sometimes, hard work will be required of us, if we want to do what the Father has called us to do. We can work hard and at the same time be at rest in our hearts because we have been delivered from the pressure to perform. Jesus has done it all on the cross and we can be at rest in His accomplishment.

Finding Rest for Our Souls

Come to Me, all who are weary and burdened, and I will give you rest. Take My yoke upon you and learn from Me, for I am gentle and humble in heart, and you will find rest for your souls. For My yoke is comfortable, and My burden is light (Matt. 11:28-30 NASB).

Jesus says that in His presence, we find rest for our souls. This is one of the benefits of the new covenant. When we are at home in His presence, resting will become a lifestyle. I remember how my perspective on rest changed as I discovered the new covenant. Ever since I got saved, I always carried a longing to live fully for Jesus. I was very zealous but I lacked insight of the grace of God. I was driven to try to please God and to become the best disciple possible. My motivation was not bad. I loved God and longed to live a lifestyle of obedience, but because I lacked revelation of the finished work of Jesus Christ, I could never find the true rest of faith. I thought that making my life with God work was up to me and that expanding the Kingdom of God hinged on my efforts. I gave it my best but failed miserably. It was then that the Holy Spirit started to unveil to me what Jesus had done through His redemptive work on the cross. I realized that what I had tried to accomplish by my own strength, He had already accomplished for me. I didn't have to strive to become a perfect disciple, because He had already sanctified and made me complete and perfect in Him. The Holy Spirit revealed to me that *"…we are sanctified through the offering of the body of Jesus Christ once for all…. For by one offering he hath perfected forever them that are sanctified"* (Hebr. 10:10, 14). Understanding this led me into a lifestyle of rest.

Rest Is the Flavor of Faith

Therefore, we must fear if, while a promise remains of entering His rest, any one of you may seem to have come short of it. For indeed we have had good news preached to us, just as they also did; but the word they heard did not benefit them, because they were not united with those who listened with faith. For we who have believed enter that rest (Hebr. 4:1-3 NASB).

We enter the rest of the new covenant by faith. When we hear and believe the gospel, rest will always come as a fruit. Hearing the gospel does not mean hearing messages about what we need to do for Jesus, neither does it mean hearing how to live as good believers. These are fruits of the transforming work of the love of God in our lives. Hearing the good news of the gospel means hearing about what Jesus has already accomplished for us on the cross. As we find out what He has done for us and receive it by faith, we will find rest in Christ. Therefore, rest is the flavor and manifestation of faith. The main reason for a lot of the stress and striving among believers today is unbelief. If a believer hears the gospel, but for some reason doesn't believe it, living at rest with Christ becomes impossible. The true rest of faith always comes from a revelation of the gospel.

Taking Time to Rest

Knowing that there is no longer any requirement for us to strive to please God makes it much easier to put times of rest into our schedule. After all, it is hard to be at rest in our relationship with God if we live with the belief that everything depends on how well we perform. As we're growing in our understanding of how the new covenant, we will find that the pressure of Kingdom work has never been on our shoulders. Jesus Himself is building His church and He knows what He is doing. He does not need our efforts to fulfill His purposes, but He really enjoys building together with us, so He has invited us to participate in what He is doing. Since Jesus is the one in charge, we can take some time off every now and then without having to worry that we are missing out on the will of God.

The Sabbath as a Prophetic Picture

The sabbath was an important day in Israel. *"Six days shall work be done: but the seventh day is the sabbath of rest, an holy convocation;*

ye shall do no work therein: it is the sabbath of the LORD in all your dwellings" (Lev. 23:3). The sabbath was their holy day of rest and keeping it was considered to be an act of obedience and worship. This is because it pleases our Father when we take time to rest. In the Old Covenant it was seen as a serious trespass to break the sabbath, even punishable by death. *"Six days may work be done; but in the seventh is the sabbath of rest, holy to the LORD: whosoever doeth any work in the sabbath day, he shall surely be put to death" (Exodus 31:15).* The truth is that the sabbath is a prophetic picture of our life of resting in Christ. Paul writes: *"So let no one judge you in food or in drink, or regarding a festival or a new moon or sabbaths, which are a shadow of things to come, but the substance is of Christ" (Col. 2:16-17 NKJV).* Jesus Christ is the fulfillment of the sabbath day, and in Him we can now live in a constant state of rest. Jesus Himself is our sabbath. However, it is still a very good idea to have a free day every week where we take time to rest. This is not just a law that the people in the old covenant was required to keep. It is a spiritual principle given for our good so that we can stay well rested and refreshed.

The Sabbath was Made for Man

"And he said unto them, The sabbath was made for man, and not man for the sabbath: therefore the Son of man is Lord also of the sabbath" (Mark 2:27-28).

The sabbath was given to us because our Father knows that we need rest, and that learning how to rest is an important aspect of our life with God. We even read earlier that when Jesus invites us to come to Him, His intention is to provide rest for our souls. The many conflicts that arose between Jesus and the pharisees concerning Him healing people on the sabbath was because they had gotten this backwards. In their thinking, man had been made to keep the sabbath. They put the act of keeping the sabbath at the center, not the love and compassion of God. Jesus gave the sabbath as an invitation for us to rest and be refreshed. We need that if we are going to stay healthy and happy. You can always discern when you have shifted into a performance-based way of thinking by checking if the disciplines have replaced the heart of God as the center of your spiritual life.

The Love of the Father at the Center

It is always important to keep the main thing as the main thing. We need to remember that the main thing is to remain grounded and rooted in the love of the Father and to keep living loved by Him as our foundation. To build our relationship with God never comes down to performing rituals to gain His favor, or how well we perform the spiritual disciplines mentioned throughout these pages. Abiding in the Father's love and living out of the finished work of Christ is always our foundation. Spiritual disciplines, including resting, is very valuable as ways of responding to Him who loved us first, but they are never the main thing. The main thing is to keep on living loved by Him and to make His love and grace known everywhere (1 John 4:16-19).

Finding Peace in His Presence

I am leaving you with a gift—peace of mind and heart. And the peace I give is a gift the world cannot give. So don't be troubled or afraid (John 14:27 NLT).

Jesus promised to give us His peace and being at peace in mind and heart has a lot to do with us being able to rest. Since rest is not the same as inactivity, we need a better definition of what rest is. Maybe one of the best ways of defining rest is to say that *resting means being at peace in the presence of God.* In His presence we find harmony and there we are being revived and renewed. Resting is a form of spiritual warfare as well. It is no coincidence that Paul wrote: *"And the God of peace will crush Satan under your feet shortly. The grace of our Lord Jesus Christ be with you. Amen"* (Rom. 16:20 NKJV). Being filled with the peace of God is powerful because Satan has no weapon against it. Satan always operates in stress and fear, but when someone is full of God's peace, the works of the devil will be exposed and his plans will fail.

My Habits of Resting

We read earlier how the author of Hebrews encourages us to *"… make every effort to enter that rest, so that no one will fall by following the same example of disobedience"* (Hebr. 4:11 NASB). It takes some effort to plan for rest, because being active and working for God comes so naturally for many of us, while resting proves to be much more challenging. To make sure that I am not negating my times or rest, I have developed some habits that have proven helpful. I want to share some of them here as an encouragement and help for you:

- I have made it a habit of resting one day every week. During this day I don't work. It is sometimes hard not to read my e-mails or answer work related phone calls on my days off, but it has become easier through the years. The time we take for rest and refreshing is always time well spent. It will help us to have the strength to keep on walking with God for many years to come.

- I never open my mail, read messages, or make any work-related phone calls until after I have spent quality time with the Father, Son and Holy Spirit every morning.

- During the summer I try to keep at least four weeks free from traveling and preaching in conferences. I try to do the same at the end of the year as well. Again, this is not always easy because I love to be active, to preach and to meet people, but I have realized that I am a much better husband, father, preacher, writer and friend when I am well rested.

- Another important key for me has been learning how to be mentally present when I'm at home. This used to be a big challenge for me. Since I was traveling to so many nations in the world, it was easy for me to be mentally present at the mission field, even while being at home. This became very frustrating for my wife and kids, so I realized that I needed to do something to change this. Over time I have developed a habit that have helped me and it looks something like this: As I am on my way back from a mission trip, I take some time during the trip to evaluate what has happened and then I leave the trip in the hands of God. I then turn my focus and attention to my wife and kids so that when they meet me at the airport, I am fully with them. That has helped me to be present, not only physically but also in mind and heart.

- Another important habit for me has been to make sure that I do the things that I enjoy and help me to rest. I enjoy watching sports or a good movie, spending time with my family and playing video games with my kids. I also really enjoy reading books or listen to podcasts. I try to make sure to plan my schedule, so that I have the time to do this. It helps me to be at rest and live in peace.

We all have different schedules and life situations to handle, so I am not suggesting that you plan your times of rest the same way as I do. I share these points with you as an encouragement to find ways that will be helpful to you as you plan your free time.

What Happens When We Don't Live in Rest?

Isaiah gives a prophetic statement about what will happen when the people of God reject the resting place that the Father offers. *"He who said to them, 'This is the place of quiet, give rest to the weary,' and, 'This is the resting place,' yet they would not listen" (Isa. 28:12 AMP).* They were offered a place to rest but they wouldn't listen. At times we can fall into this same trap and it doesn't even have to be a conscious choice. Life moves at a high pace for so many of us and we can be so caught up with the busyness of it all that we cannot hear the voice of God when He is telling us to slow down. When life moves at a high pace, it is much harder to hear the signals that our body tries to give us about our need for rest. Isaiah reveals the consequences of missing our place of rest as he continues his prophetic declaration:

"Therefore the word of the Lord to them will be [merely monotonous repetitions]: 'Precept upon precept, precept upon precept, Rule upon rule, rule upon rule, Here a little, there a little.' That they may go and stumble backward, and be broken, ensnared, and taken captive" (Isa. 28:13 AMP).

Our life with God will become a religious performance and monotonous repetition if we forget to rest in Christ. Therefore, we need to listen to the advice that we read in Hebrews and strive to enter the rest of faith. That will set the Word of God ablaze in our heart by the fire of His burning love.

How to Build a Lifestyle of Rest

Jesus is now our sabbath rest. True peace is always found in our relationship with Him. By knowing Jesus, we learn to live out of the rest that He brings. There are certain steps that we can take and some priorities that we can make that will help us in doing that. Here are some of the principles that have helped me:

1. **Being Established in the New Covenant.**
    As we have seen earlier in this chapter, internal rest will
    be the fruit of having insight into the New Covenant. As
    we realize that everything that God requires of us, have
    already been fulfilled by Jesus Christ, we find rest in His
    accomplishment. This will lead us to embrace a lifestyle
    of rest and peace.

2. **Realize that You Are Not the Solution to Everything.**
    Knowing that Jesus is the one who is building His church
    releases us from a lot of pressure. When we are resting,
    He keeps building His church, and He does it very well.
    We find a lot of freedom and peace by realizing that we
    are not so important that His work to build the church
    stops just because we take some time off.

3. **Planning for Vacation and Days of Rest.**
    We have already looked at this earlier, but it's well worth
    mentioning once again. Life is so busy and full of stress,
    that if we don't make plans to rest it will not happen. I
    suggest that you take time monthly, just to sit down and
    write days and times of rest into your schedule for the
    following month. If it works better for you, you could do
    it on a weekly basis as well.

4. **Allow Other People to Check Your Schedule.**
    We can sometimes be blind to how fast paced our lives
    have become. I like to stay active and I am a very goal-
    oriented person, so I tend to be a little bit too optimistic
    with my time. To protect me from succumbing to that
    weakness, it has been helpful for me to allow my wife
    and kids to be part of my planning. Sometimes discuss it
    with my mentors as well. The people that are close to
    you can see things that you are not seeing. Their input

can provide some very valuable help. So, my suggestion is that you allow them to weigh in on how you plan your time.

CLOSING WORDS

I wrote this book to highlight some of the ways through which we can partner with Jesus Christ to build a dynamic relationship with Him. All these spiritual disciplines are found in the Bible, and I have seen the need for teaching on this topic from a new covenant perspective. Life becomes boring if we live in passivity, so finding ways to respond to the Father is an important part of our life as His children. I have personally benefited a lot from the habits and disciplines that we have studied throughout this book. They have helped me to respond to the love of God and to grow in intimacy with the Holy Spirit. I hope they will be a help and a blessing for you as well.

The truth is that if we want to live a lifestyle of abiding in the love of God, we need good habits and commitment to spiritual disciplines. This has nothing to do with being legalistic, but it has everything to do with guarding the fire in our hearts that has been set ablaze by the love of the Father. Spiritual disciplines and good habits are ways in which we partner with Jesus so that his life can be formed within us. The goal is to learn to love like Jesus did. Jesus always revealed the love of the Father and as we partner with Him, we will be conformed into His image so that our lives reveal the love of the Father everywhere we go.

But now, as we have reached the last pages of this book, we need to come back to the most important thing, which is abiding in the love of the Father. That is the purpose of everything. He wants us to know Him and to be rooted and grounded in His love. I want to end this book by pointing us back to the scripture that has inspired me to write this book and in fact, the whole series that this book is a part of.

And we have known and believed the love that God has for us. God is love, and he who abides in love abides in God, and God in him. Love has been perfected among us in this: that we may have boldness in the day of judgment; because as He is, so are we in this world. There is no fear in love; but perfect love casts out fear, because fear involves torment. But he who fears has not been made perfect in love. We love Him because He first loved us (1 John 4:16-19 NKJV).

Abiding in the Father's love, being transformed by His love, yes, even being consumed by His love, so that we reflect His heart to the world, that is our purpose in life. Our calling is to learn to be good receivers of His love, goodness and grace. Every good habit and spiritual discipline that we're practicing building the secret place with Him is meant to be an expression of that.

The love of Jesus is like burning fire. It has a wildness to it. His love raises up pioneers that break with status quo and the dead traditions of religion. The next book in this series will be called *"The Burning Love of Jesus Christ"*. In that book we will continue studying how we can abide in the love of God, but there we will look at it from the perspective of being the bride of Christ. The story of Jesus and His bride is the romance of the ages. His love makes us bold, so that we dare to tread on paths and travel on roads where we have never walked before.

There are probably a lot of things that could be written as a final encouragement, but I think that the best way to end this book is by leaving you with these words:

Your Father loves you, and He is well pleased with you!

BIBLIOGRAPHY

Unless otherwise indicated, all scriptural quotations are from the *King James Version* of the Bible.

Scripture references marked AMP are taken from Amplified® Bible Copyright © 2015 by The Lockman Foundation, La Habra, CA 90631.

Scripture references marked The Message are taken from The Message. Copyright © 1993, 1994, 1995, 1996, 2000, 2001, 2002.

Scripture references marked NASB are taken from NEW AMERICAN STANDARD BIBLE® NASB® Copyright © 1960, 1971, 1977,1995, 2020 by The Lockman Foundation A Corporation Not for Profit La Habra, CA All Rights Reserved.

Scripture references marked NIV are taken from the HOLY BIBLE, NEW INTERNATIONAL VERSION®. NIV®. Copyright © 1973, 1978, 1984 by the International Bible Society.

Scripture quotations marked NLT are taken from the Holy Bible, New Living Translation, copyright 1996, 2004, 2007, 2015 by Tyndale House Foundation. Used by permission of Tyndale House Publishers, Inc., Carol Stream, Illinois 60188. All rights reserved.

Scripture references marked NKJV are taken from The Holy Bible, New King James Version, Copyright © 1982 Thomas Nelson. All rights reserved.

Scripture references marked TPT are taken from The Passion Translation® is a registered trademark of Passion & Fire Ministries, Inc. Copyright © 2020 Passion & Fire Ministries, Inc.

ABOUT THE AUTHOR

Martin Reén lives in the north of Sweden together with His wife Linda and their three children Isak, Benjamin and Noomi. Martin's and Linda's vision has always been to get to know the heart of the Father in deeper ways, to grow in intimacy with Jesus Christ and to be conformed into His image. Martin's vision is to introduce as many parts of the body of Christ as possible to the love of the Father and the finished work of Jesus Christ, so that the believers can be secure in their identity as sons and daughters of God and learn to live by the life of Christ. Martin and Linda travel all over the world to preach the gospel and teach in Bible schools, seminars, conferences and on-line events. They work with missions, counselling and leadership training as well.